Billy Childish was born in 1959 in Chatham, Kent, and left school at sixteen. After working in Chatham Naval Dockyard as an apprentice stonemason, he went on to study painting, which proved to be unsatisfactory.

Billy Childish was diagnosed dyslexic at the age of 28. Despite this, he has published more than thirty poetry collections and three novels. He has recorded over one hundred albums on a variety of independent record labels and exhibited paintings all over the world.

Other Books by Billy Childish

Fiction
My Fault
Sex Crimes of the Futcher

Poetry
Companions in a Death Boat
Days With a Hart Like a Dog
Poems to Break the Harts of Impossible Princesses
Big Hart and Balls
In 5 Minits You'll Know Me
'I'd rather you lied.' Selected Poems 1980–1998
Chatham Town Welcomes Desperate Men

Billy's Website: www.hangmanbooks.com

NOTEBOOKS OF A NAKED YOUTH

by Billy Childish

This edition published in 2005 by
Virgin Books Ltd
Thames Wharf Studios
Rainville Road
London W6 9HA

First published in 1997 by Codex Books

Woodcuts by Billy Childish

Typeset by Phoenix Photosetting, Chatham, Kent
Printed and bound by Mackays of Chatham Ltd, Kent

ISBN 0 7535 1017 0

A word about Notebooks of a Naked Youth

Read this. It will not only make you laugh till you've got tears in your eyes, it will require you to carry on weeping till you burst out laughing again. *Notebooks of a Naked Youth* is a wicked, funny, preposterous book of gigantic scope and power, stunningly important like all of Billy Childish's work, and so tough to describe that I can only urge everyone with an interest in the contemporary scene to beg, borrow, buy, or otherwise hijack a copy immediately.

Meanwhile, the Childish saga hobbles onward, stiff-trousered with the fly forever bursting and leaking as always, and even more pustular about the gob than usual. It's a comedy of course, or a tragedy, depending whether or not the reader enjoys a brazen order of lust, equipped with drip-dry boils, razor blades and shiny red shoes. Or, like Billy's narrator himself, wrestles alone in bed or under the bedpan with the canons of giant art.

Michael Baldwin, 1997

The breath of my father

And Jacob was left alone; and there a man wrestled with him until the breaking of the day. When the man saw that he did not prevail against Jacob, he touched the hollow of his left thigh; and Jacob's thigh was put out of joint as he wrestled with him.

Then he said, 'Let me go for the day is breaking.' But Jacob said, 'I will not let you go, unless you bless me.' And he said to him, 'What is your name?' 'Jacob.' Then he said, 'Your name shall no longer be called Jacob, but Israel, for you have striven with God and with men, and you have prevailed.'

GENESIS 32, verses 24–28

BOOK ONE

I still thieve and I still lie, and I admire myself and admonish myself pitilessly. My name, by the way, is not important and I shall not disclose it to you. All you need to know is that I was born in such-and-such a town to a pair of so-and-so's and I have no brothers or sisters, with the exception of one brother.

Actually my name is William Loveday, but it's down to you whether you choose to believe me or not. I come from a long line of illustrious Lovedays, all of them alcoholics, dandies and sodomites.

The landlady left a note under my door last night informing me that I have loud feet, disagreeable friends, a ridiculous haircut and should vacate the premises by the end of the month. Which is all hogwash!

I screwed the note up and tossed it into my provisions box/waste paper basket, which contains half a packet of digestive biscuits, some ginseng tea and a packet of monkey nuts, as I'd already eaten the green grapes during the night.

Tomorrow, or the day after, I will bunk the train to London, attend the Academy for the afternoon and collect my term's grant cheque, then I shall be rich!

Of course, going to art college is silly and immature but

then again it isn't. Our head tutor is soft and flabby and Mister Bennet is hard and arrogant. It will take all of my self-control not to imagine punching him in the teeth and knocking him arse-first down two flights of stairs.

If you jut your whole torso out through my bedroom window and crank your head round sideways, you can just make out the Jewish cemetery over the wall. Which means the whole street is probably haunted.

Over the road is the pub and behind that is the river. The river is what dominates this town. One day I shall walk down to its dockside, climb onto a passing boat, hire out my services and never come back. That's what I tell myself. I kid myself that I'm brave and adventurous, which of course I am.

Every night the fog climbs into my room and smothers me with its melancholy and then I wonder about myself, about my past and my uncertain future, and I wonder if I have anything to be happy about or to look forward to, and then I go to my rotten suitcase, pull out my men's magazines and masturbate.

All of this will change when I come to be in charge. The tutors at our Academy seem to believe that they have the right to sleep with all of the young female students regardless – by holy birthright! Which, in my opinion, is an abuse of their position and power. What's more, I know for a fact that Mister Bennet is jealous of me, jealous of my talent and the fact that I am going to be a big hit with his lousy ladies!

Another original idea, seeing as that's what everybody wants, is to start using a drinking glass upside down.

'But the water will be in your lap!' you shout.

'Sir, I am quite aware of your idiotic suggestions, but it is still somehow different, wouldn't you say? And, as we all know, what really counts is a first-class brain, with the intelligence to show us that a house brick isn't really a house brick at all, but rather something quite inexplicably different.'

Another idea is to use invisible paintbrushes and to only draw on the back of the canvas – but this would be stupid and facetious.

The scariest thing about ghosts is – if you know who they are or you don't know them at all. What would terrify me the most is if my father just walked in here glowing with his peroxide hair, his little blond beard and glistening moustache. Some nights I can almost smell the brandy on his breath, then I have to leave this room and cross the high street to the pub. And, once there, force myself to drink out of pure spite. And I buy cigarettes just for the thrill of spending money I can't afford and so's I know that I am ruining my health and it's all because of my mother and the way that I have been brought up, and I feel secure in the knowledge that I am sacrificing myself for those who have gone before me.

This morning I had a hangover, hot pimples on the tip of my tongue, a sore throat and ulcers. As it happens, I spat blood. I cleaned my teeth so vigorously that I ripped my gum and yelped.

I have been lying on this stinking old mattress listening to my heartbeat. First I could hear something thumping in my head, then I imagined I could hear my heart, which probably I couldn't. Then I noticed a slight tremor under my left eye. Every thirty or so seconds I can feel the skin twitch, which is something to do with the liver. I know this because I heard it from a Chinese and, as everybody knows, they are experts on such matters.

The skin on my fingers and thumbs is dry and peeling off again; the pharmacist tells me that it is perfectly normal and that everybody sheds their skin once every two years. I have a tube of cream, which I rub into my hands. I also use it on the foreskin of my cock; the skin there is dry and I can't pull it back on account of I am dirty, lazy and ashamed. Actually, I'm scared. I masturbated three times since yesterday and the skin split and there was a little blood.

My father has lumps in the centre of both of his palms which is a sure sign that his liver's completely fucked and sooner or later he will have to become a ghost.

One of the funnier things I've been accused of is helping completely innocent people to look somehow stupid, for which I should most probably feel ashamed . . . I've said that all back to front and used all the 'wrong type' of words. How I hate to use the 'right type' of words.

It is important to establish your own style, but then again it isn't. Far more important, but then again not, is to be liked. But no matter what, you can't deny that above all else, one should at least try to be polite and refrain from petty criticism or downright sarcasm. 'Sarcasm,' as my mother was always pointing out, 'is the lowest form of wit'. Which is true. 'But it is also the funniest,' I added cheekily. She dropped the potato knife heavily into the sink and gave me a black look, to let me know that she would never ever love me again and I danced out the room laughing and feeling very pleased with myself.

That's something the old dears love – a cheeky chappie! Just so long as he's not outright rude or crude, or at least not obviously so. Not to be heavy-handed – that's what counts, unless of course you're dealing with the ignorant because, no matter what else you might say, you can't repeat yourself too many times for the dull-witted.

'You have to learn to read and write!' my mother kept repeating, which I didn't believe at all.

'Why?' I asked.

'So you can . . . er, so you can . . . so you don't have to ask for the toilet!' she said triumphantly.

My father is a mystery to me and I never talk of him. It seems silly and a little bit cheeky to write things down and pretend that it's the truth. Everybody hates a tell-tale-tit, and even with the best intentions at heart we can never quite be sure if what we're putting down isn't just a pack of lies intended to befuddle old women and keep arrogant young men from accosting us in the streets.

Only if my father comes up in the conversation do I deem to mention him, and then only to ridicule him. To let people know that I'm not so stupid and can look after myself when it comes to belittling others.

One thing is true – everybody hates my pathetic poetry and my whole family, and all of my so-called friends are of the opinion that I should shut my big cake-hole!

Just because my father has the appearance of an Edwardian spook, it would be improper to infer from this alone that in a previous life he was some kind of perfumed gentleman or, as has been suggested by some of his more vocal girlfriends, 'a tyrannical dandy and unmitigated shit of quite devastating proportions!'

For sure, my father is guilty as sin but I think that even the liberals amongst you would agree that it is unfair to hang a man entirely on his appearance, even if various ugly rumours pertaining to his skullduggery and base behaviour have been circulating in polite society, and his name has appeared in the courts.

Dangerous poisonous toadstools are fairly common in woodland and could easily be confused with a harmless edible mushroom, with alarming consequences.

If my father, for example, was to accidentally ingest even half a cap of a Destroying Angel the results could be quite serious.

Symptoms appear in two phases, separated by a period of apparent recovery which can be very misleading. In the first phase the digestive system is affected, with symptoms appearing in 6–24 hours; these include dryness of the mouth, vomiting, abdominal pain and diarrhoea, often with blood. These initial symptoms can be very severe, and last as long as 24 hours, after which they subside, and for up to three days it can appear that the patient has recovered. During this period, however, severe liver and kidney damage is taking place. Further symptoms then become apparent, with weakness, jaundice and general deterioration often culminating in delirium, convulsions, unconsciousness, and death.

Poisoning has occurred under natural conditions in goats, and experimentally in dogs, but in general little is known about the effects of this fungus on domestic animals.

Medical treatment is required urgently, as it is effective only in the early stages before irreversible liver and kidney damage occurs.

Note: *This fungus is extremely dangerous, even very small quantities can cause death.*

I know it's silly to write things down, but it's also good and important, though a little arrogant and pointless. Actually it's sinful. What makes it most compelling is that there's something cheeky in writing down complete, downright lies and letting po-faced judges believe every word of it, like as if it was gospel – not of course that I'd ever intentionally tell a lie.

Next week I am going to change my name by deed poll, which is perfectly legal and binding. I have spoken to somebody at the Social Security office and they've advised me to see a solicitor, which I shall do when I am good and ready.

I stole one of my father's collars and a bow tie for my interview at the dole office and I didn't stammer or blush once.

'I'm looking for something in the Arts,' I venture.

'And have you any qualifications?' she questions me.

I look at this madam, sat there in her ridiculous dress and spectacles.

'I will be qualified,' I assure her.

'You do understand that it is illegal to be in full-time education and claim benefit at the same time?' she says, not being able to control herself from spitting.

'The way people talk to each other is out of all proportion to their positions,' I announce.

She stares at me and writes something down on my file which I can't quite read.

I've been unemployed since before last summer. Before that I was in the dockyard and before that I was still in school.

Naturally, I have no inclination to work and, without a hint of arrogance, I can fairly say that I am in a class of my own.

Work, for some people, is their life's blood – they long to be bossed from morning to night; to be paid to sit around gassing and scarcely lifting a finger, but always available; always at the beck and call of the boss man. Whereas I, on the other hand, have an independent streak and love to feel hungry, to lie here in this little six quid a week room listening to my murmuring heart and the junkies in the basement planning their next robbery.

Friday:
I have been practising my new signature today.

Shall I get a job soon? I hope not. As far as teachers were concerned, I refuse to knuckle down, grow up, or have any of my rough corners knocked off.

'Grow up!' People have been shouting that one at me for years, but if a young writer isn't ready for something then he just isn't ready. I have stated my preference and that should be an end to it.

Yesterday I had a man interview me at the dole office instead of the usual old harpy.

'The times they are a-changing,' he said to me in a silly theatrical way. Then he raised his eyebrows and made a great show of wrinkling up his forehead and thinking. I had the distinct impression of some wise old owl who had taken it upon himself to teach an unruly fledgling right from wrong. In fact, he made me feel like an ill-mannered schoolboy and I made a rude sign at him in my pocket.

I was wearing my father's starched collar and bow tie in an endeavour to make myself totally unemployable. I had also scrubbed my hands and sat studying my cuticles in a delicate and refined way, as I imagine elderly gentlemen might do in old films.

He told me that at least I had the courage to look him in the eye.

'Not like some of the rubbish I get coming in here!' He says pointedly, 'This new government is looking for a crackdown on benefit scroungers and defrauders.'

I look up at him. 'A short sharp shock?' I venture helpfully.

He narrows his eyes at me, then shuffles his files and asks me to sign some papers, which is a good opportunity for me to practise my new signature.

If it so happened that I was awakened in the middle of the night and dragged from my bed by a lynch mob, who then took it into their feeble minds to bind, gag and garrotte me, then fling my shuddering corpse to its watery grave in an old dyke. Then, most likely I would lay there face down for the next seven thousand or so years, drinking mud to my heart's content. And then, if by chance, one day, in the impossible future, a little girl should happen along, it would hardly come as a surprise if, after lying there water-logged for all those centuries, I didn't just pull myself up from all that slime, reach out my clawed fist for her passing white ankle and, if she screamed out in alarm (as young girls are apt to do), perhaps it would also be quite understandable if I then pulled her down into that mire in an attempt to placate her and stifle her incessant cries. And, more than likely, I would hold onto and treasure one of her beautiful shiny red shoes, slobbering wet mud all over it, kissing it and clasping it to my muddy bosom.

Shortly I will start work on my poem. I have bought a brand new notebook especially for this purpose. I have also taken a set of new photographs in the photo booths in The Pentagon Shopping Centre, from which I am going to choose one for the cover of my book. I am wearing a white silk scarf and my face is all at once sad and sullen.

No one in this building knows who I really am, which is exciting, but at the same time they do. One good thing is that the landlady doesn't recognise me and has forgotten about her threat to have me thrown out.

When I sell my story and leave this fleapit, I will send a

full-page exposé to all the papers, letting them know exactly what I think of her miserly money-grabbing nature. Evidently she is a member of the bourgeoisie.

I have selected a different photo for the cover of my book. In it I am wearing my tweed jacket and have such an unbelievable look of pain in my eyes that it will make girls want to weep for me. I have an unbelievably romantic nature, which no one must ever see or come to know about. If people are to find out, it will be only in secret and bit-by-bit.

Lately my mind has been running off in all manner of unexpected directions. It's quite true to say that my mind is like a cesspool but, even after taking this into consideration, I still think myself superior in every way to my pathetic equals. It's also true to say that somebody will have to pay for all the insults and injuries that have been perpetrated against me by my so-called teachers in the name of education. Or rather they won't. Who knows? If the mood so takes me then maybe I will choose to hurt them.

Of course, some sceptics will call a man who sees black panthers on the loose in the English countryside (or our 'garden of Kent' as some fat-heads still insist on calling it) a half-wit. Or, even more insultingly, feeble-minded, which is rude and a quite unnecessary tone to take with a young writer who is merely doing his uppermost to report the facts as they occur to him. And, knowing for sure that black panthers are indeed at large in this city of ours, it is only reasonable to presume that by now at least one of them will probably have turned itself into a ghost and will have decided to spend its time prowling through the twilight hours stalking shadows and imaginary prey. And if one of these panther spirits were to decide to track me remorselessly in its nocturnal wanderings, it would also come as no surprise to be able to hear its extended claws clicking on the pavement as it follows behind me. And so it is with me ever since I first clapped eyes on that black beast which crossed my path in broad daylight some six years ago.

One thing I love to do is to waste money needlessly. Another is to always have some little stash hidden away for a rainy day and not tell anybody about it; to egg people on; to make believe I'm poor when all the while I have fifteen pounds safely stitched inside the lining of my old greatcoat; to stand around in bus queues rattling bits of old change around in my pocket then to pull five pounds out when people are least expecting it; to live from hand to mouth for months on end, really starving myself like a winter sparrow and then to throw all caution to the wind and spend all my money on Moroccan cigars like there's no tomorrow.

To be a hero is what counts, but to be broken down and wretched as well, and to get strange women talking about you and thinking about you . . . Above all else, to remain a mystery!

I step out into this low winter sunlight, find an empty doorway and rip my special author's notebook from its brown paper bag. I lick my pencil and write: 'The Idiocy of Ideas' on the front of the book in a bold and imposing style. I print my name and address underneath, then ponder whether to add the country as England or the UK . . . I decide on Great Britain. I chew on my tongue and engrave it into the cover. I hold it up to the light and read it over three or four times in my mind, trying to stop my lips from moving. There is no doubt that it is a very auspicious beginning to a classic piece of prose. I take my pencil and cross out 'Great Britain' in great vicious swathes and write 'england' in its place – england with a small 'e'. Then I turn the first page and practise writing my signature.

I try it with and without initials. I write it crossways, from top to bottom and from bottom to top. In the end I have more swirls under my name than even Elizabeth I.

Blank pages have always put the fear of God into me. I turn the page and sit there biting on my pencil, but refuse to write down any of my wonderful ideas. Then suddenly I dash off the date in a single flourish and just crouch there, my arse getting cold, my brain empty and my energy completely spent. I check to see if I have any thoughts whatsoever, which I haven't.

I'm empty, so why write? Perhaps an earwig unwittingly sauntered into your ear in your sleep and, having no malicious motives whatsoever but apparently nothing better to do, has decided to hollow your brains clean out.

Actually, the thing that really keeps me from writing anything down is the fear that if I ever do write my book then maybe I will be compelled, out of some peculiar superstition, to write another one and then another one, and so on, and so forth, until I would have to become a disgusting professional who writes 'beautifully crafted lines'. In short, there would be no end to it.

My friends at the Academy think I am a fool, and if I say anything that contradicts them, they disprove me by saying that what I say is only words.

Actually, none of my friends particularly like me and I don't particularly like them either. Or rather, we're not possessed of the bravery necessary to descend into the depths of our own rancid souls, which in truth is the only place where we will ever be able to find the similarities that bind us, and therefore the answers to our fears and prejudices, and then begin on the road to understanding and forgiving one another.

We really do our best to appear jovial and good-natured, but the jokes we tell at each other's expense, our jibes and playful teasings, all this is really just a ruse to keep each other's big traps shut and to smash a mug down and keep the dirty upstart in his place, to make absolutely sure that he has the right haircut and doesn't get any big ideas above his station.

The important thing is not to blush; to be funny and not to show any weakness; to keep our emotions hidden to our chests like a hand of cards. Then you might at least have a chance of winning, and might be able to truly smash the other fellow before he stands and is ready to fight. Which, of course, is only fair, right and proper.

Who says that my name isn't William Loveday, and by what authority do they speak? Who's to say that I wasn't one day out in the wild woods hunting with my father and brother and that I didn't somehow get myself lost on purpose, out of some sense of needing to be found, rescued and loved? And even after hearing them calling out for me for over an hour, who's to say that I didn't decide to stay hidden out of some sense of spite towards them and myself? And then, as night fell, wouldn't it be quite reasonable for me to climb into the hollow of a great tree and cover myself with strips of bark and handfuls of old leaves so as to keep myself warm through that cold forest's night? And wouldn't it also be perfectly possible that unbeknownst to myself I had holed up in the lair of some great and fearful bear that would come snuffling for me in the dark hours of night? And bug-eyed and terrified I would have to look on whilst it devoured my stomach and intestines in its vile salivating jaws. And in just such a situation it would be quite normal, don't you think, for my spirit to leave my body and rise up into the branches of that tree from where it might perch and look down to see that great furry head ripping out the contents of my poor belly?

Next day I would see one of the villagers come by and, seeing the bear stood over the husk of my corpse, he would run and go fetch my father and brother who would come with other villagers bearing torches and sticks and would brutally kill that poor bear, before solemnly collecting my remains, placing them on a litter and dragging them back to our village.

And then, as their voices died away into the distance, I imagine that my spirit would be quite at home living in that tree. And over the years, it would almost certainly become something of a tree spirit itself, until some five or six years later the tree would be blown down in a great gale and my spirit would be summoned by the village witch doctor, who would have to be wearing the skin of the bear who ate my stomach, and in his hand he would shake a rattle, full of the teeth of that gruesome beast.

And so, from that calling, I would have to enter my village for one last time and see my father and brother picked out in the fire-light as my spirit and the spirit of the bear were finally released, and I would soar up into the cosmos and look back at this strangely-glowing blue planet.

I get collared for stealing a jar of hair-gel from Boots the Chemist in Chatham. A woman store detective arrests me in the street and I'm taken to a small back room and searched in the presence of a police officer. I recognise him at once as Inspector Sorrel, a broken-down beat sergeant with a vendetta against poets and young writers in general. He bristles his moth-eaten moustache at me and welcomes me with open arms. Actually, he thinks that the whole incident is hilarious.

'What, may I ask, were you going to do with a jar of Country Born setting gel?'

'Spike my hair,' I say moronically.

'So you can look like a drowned rat?' He smirks. 'Why not pay for it like everybody else? It only costs 46-and-a-half-pence!' He laughs, spittle flying from his lips.

I stare at the thick crust of dandruff that completely eclipses his epaulettes.

'I didn't steal it,' I say tiredly, 'I've got the money in my pocket, I'll pay for it now.'

'Oh no you won't!' he snaps. 'You'll pay for it later, in court. Along with all the other villains in this stinking town!'

With that he handcuffs me and leads me through the streets to the police station. He takes great delight in going the long way round, leading me in front of the angry shoppers and pulling at my chain as if I am a mongrel dog who needs to be brought to heel.

Finally we arrive at the nick and he shows me to my room, which, in my humble opinion, is very poorly decorated. He slings me in there, locks the door and saunters off.

They keep me cooped up in that piss-smelling shit-hole for the whole afternoon whilst Sorrel argues the toss about my bail and who's going to fill in my charge sheet.

I have to kick on that door quite hard to even get a sip of water out of those tight bastards and even then they make me say please and thank you. I take the opportunity to explain to that turnkey that I absolutely refuse to spend another moment in that horrible room!

'I'd rather spend the night on the street!' I spit. He looks at me suspiciously and I can tell that I've hurt his feelings, for which I am extremely sorry. I step forward, take his hand in mine and promise from now on to be a model prisoner.

'It's true that the decorations are a little Spartan, but on the whole they are to my liking. It's also true to say that the walls are smeared with the excrement of foul gutter-snipes, but all in all I have no complaints. The bench is a trifle on the hard side and at home we don't have bars on the windows, but that is a minor detail. A small wash stand, a bar of soap, a towel and hot water would not go amiss ... but that's not to say that I'm at all dissatisfied, you understand. Probably I deserve no better and it would be quite understandable if you decide to turf me out of my lovely cell and throw me into your deepest and darkest dungeon!'

But instead of embracing me, the turnkey jumps back from my warm advance and emits a frightened yelp, as if I had just stamped on his oafish foot rather than shared with him my most precious thoughts. Then, baring his teeth and clasping onto his ridiculous bunch of keys, he slams the cell door, bang in my face.

At about 8 o'clock, Old Sorrel comes back down the corridor rattling all the cages. He takes my dabs and a mug shot then pushes a piece of paper toward me.

'Sign it!' he barks.

'What is it?' I ask.

'The bond for your bail, sign it or stay in for the night!'

I sign and he walks me to the door.

'I'll see you in court,' he snarls.

'Good evening, officer,' I say mildly and tip my hat to him as I walk back out onto that glorious street.

I undress to my hat, socks and vest and sit in the cold on the edge of that vile stinking mattress. I pull my brother's blue, nylon sleeping bag round my feet. A total flatness pervades my entire being and I feel myself to be a windswept old skeleton without a tick of life left in him.

I look, unrecognisingly, at my emaciated reflection in the mirrored door of the wardrobe, lean forward, pull a face and 'ha' on the glass. I put my fingers in the condensation as if to stroke my neck, staring into the unknown eyes of this stranger. I kiss the cold flat glass, open mouthed, my tongue snaking about on the ice, feeling for warmth.

'What do you want?' I enquire of myself, looking into the reflection of my tired eyes. But I refuse to allow myself to be led by this silly question to which I have no answer.

I shout at myself and stare into my yellowing teeth. I grimace and snort, purposely fogging up the mirror with my hot breath, then pull a silly face and answer myself in an idiotic little voice that I scarcely recognise.

'Meeeee,' I squeak.

'Talking to yourself is stupid,' I say, subtly trying to change the subject, but I carry on bullying myself, regardless.

'Who is "meeeee"?' I cross-question myself, intent on tripping myself up and making myself a laughing stock. I rage on, shouting back and forth until I jump from the bed screaming, kick the mirror a glancing blow with my stockinged foot and yelp with pain.

There's a loud thumping on the ceiling below and I swallow my heart. I stare about me in panic then hop across the floor, climb back onto the bed and squat there, nursing my broken toe between my cold white hands.

The wardrobe door swings open and once more reveals a twisted hideous body that I don't recognise as mine; the paleness of my limbs; my hollow cheeks and the purple rings under my eyes; my teeth already tobacco stained and broken. I see myself as ugly and despise myself. I hobble to my coat pocket for my little bottle and take a sharp nip that stings from my lips to my arse and I taste vomit.

'You must become a drinker and a whore!' I say throatily to myself.

'You must grow a shell that no man can pierce, and then no woman will ever be able to hurt you again! You must grow vile and smash them all!'

I listen to myself, supping on my sour juice and then the light bulb explodes. I cower in fear in that smoky darkness. It swims around me and I mock myself ... Always to be a frightened little boy. It was so sudden and dense . . . .

I feel my way across the darkened room pawing for the light switch ... Click it back and forth – nothing! Helplessly I look for the window and feel myself begin to cry. The dirty net curtain shows pale as the moon comes from behind a purple-black cloud and I breathe again, shivering in that ice-cold air. A young writer could freeze to death on a night like this, with only a second-rate sleeping bag with its busted zip and a moth-eaten old blanket to keep him warm.

I step into my shoes, pull my jacket over my shoulders and

pick my way downstairs, through the kitchen and out into the blackness of the backyard.

'The shower is out the back,' I remember the landlady saying to me on that first day as I stood on the black and white tiles in that dirty kitchen. The whole place reeked of boiled cabbages. I had my brown cardboard suitcase by my feet and she stood there smiling to herself as she counted out my deposit – and month's rent in advance – onto the table top in front of her. All the while she kept bringing her fingers to her lips and licking at them as if they were dripping with honey.

I feel my way into the backyard and along the side wall. A door handle comes into my hand, an old-fashioned latch, I lift it and it swings into blackness. The sour stench of dirty laundry comes powerfully up to my nostrils and I enter into that damp smelling out-shed.

A sticky web draws across my face and neck. Panicking, I bang at my head and brush at myself feverishly, to knock away the fat spider that has leapt upon me.

The door whines closed behind me and what little light that was cast by the moon dies away. I stick out my hand, flailing for the light switch, then feel myself slithering down a muddy slope into a trench of ice-cold water. It comes up over my ankles and completely fills my shoes.

I bang around in the drink until I find a foothold then clamber back onto the bank. I pull off my sodden socks and shoes, slip out of my jacket and feel around for the taps. A piece of damp rope swings into my hand and I give it an experimental tug – nothing. I give it another pull and there's a 'clang!' and a great tidal wave of ice-cold water crashes down over my naked head. I gasp, my whole body contracting in pain. I blink and spit through the foam, my cock shrunk to the size of a walnut.

'No!' I gasp, 'No!' I struggle towards the door and stand in something soft and decaying and slither backwards towards the icy ditch.

My legs buckle beneath me and my head goes crashing into a shelf. I fall to the ground and lie there shivering in the mud. There's a moment's pause and then a creaking sound as the shelf above me collapses and I'm hit in the face by a rain of falling bottles. I shake my head in disbelief. I'm hit four or five times until at last the avalanche subsides. I try to pick myself up and a mop handle falls and strikes me across the bridge of the nose.

I lie there cowering, my eyes screwed tight shut, the stench of chemicals rises to my nostrils as a broken bottle glugs out its luminous contents over my belly and groin. Slowly I open my eyes and above me there shows a little square window out of which I can see the harsh outline of the Star of David on top of the synagogue next door, and the moon riding high between the stampeding, purple clouds.

My teeth start to chatter as I numbly pull myself to my feet.

My whole body shakes uncontrollably. I stand in that darkness, clutching my jacket and clothes, then slowly become aware of an intense burning sensation spreading across my thighs and balls. Screaming in agony, I throw myself back into the icy ditch.

I have decided never to leave this room again until I have written down all the names of those I've wished dead and they have come to me, one by one, and apologised to me – in person.

As for those I've killed, the armies of ants will have a place of honour at the top of my list. And, of course, my poor family and friends who I've had no respect for will be mentioned. The magical blackbird that I gunned down in the back garden will also have to be atoned for. In fact, it occurs to me that the list of blood on my hands is endless and I have decided to vacate these squalid premises at the first available opportunity. I have weighed this decision carefully in my mind and have come to the conclusion that it is the only reasonable option left open to one with such a delicate nature and refined sensibilities as myself.

My problem is that I am too accommodating by half. Even my worst enemies will tell you that I am polite to the point of painfulness and that this politeness is all too often abused by all manner of rogues and slip-shods. So this morning I will take to my bed and never get up again!

The landlady of this fleapit will also be added to my list. She is nothing less than a penny-pinching harridan. She has refused to give me a new light bulb until I have paid next month's rent – which is scandalous!

'I can't see to get in and out of bed,' I tell her.

'Well, you should've thought of that before you smashed it to bits!' she says insolently.

'Madam, I did not smash it, it exploded in my face and nearly took out my left eye! If you weren't such a skinflint you'd pay to have this worthless dump re-wired and stop playing Russian roulette with your poor lodgers' lives!'

'You pay your rent or you can get out!' she shouts, 'I'm giving you notice! You've got until the end of the week and that's it – you're out on your ear!' She turns on her heel and walks out.

After studying the miserable faces on my walk in the park this morning, I can honestly say that I was born in the wrong age and the wrong place. I belong to an entirely different time and country. A time and country where the sincere efforts of a young writer are upheld and applauded, not mocked and ridiculed. A time and country where, rather than trying to starve him to death and expose him to all manner of hardships, a young writer is given a decent bath and a light bulb when he demands it! My landlady, for one, should be punished. She is a wicked and spiteful old bag, and I have to grit my teeth and pretend I'm sucking on a sugar cube even to be able to say 'good morning' to her without spitting in her face.

It is no secret that in my endeavours to remain uneducated, it has been my father's sincerest wish that I shall be starved out of being who I am, which shall not be allowed to happen.

My father, who is a self-made man, has no time for my backwardness or insolence. 'Get an education!' he spits. Miserably, I have failed.

If one day I was to become somehow fabulously rich, I would still, nevertheless, refuse to become a professional and would instead carry on regardless, behaving like an ill-mannered youth and continue poking fun at my po-faced betters – those who at all costs must not be mocked or laughed at lest the weight, gravity and seriousness of their positions should become somehow mysteriously undermined. I say this in all seriousness, much as it is contrary to my father's dearest wishes.

In my opinion it is the professional's obsession with good taste that obliterates all creativity. It is actually this fear of life itself which forces the professional to become a neurotic expert and spitefully try to crush the intrepid amateur. And so, believing in the applause of idiots, the professional proudly obliterates all spontaneity and then, farting, sits down to lunch where, feeling pleased as punch with himself for his violence against nature, he stuffs his ignorant face, shoving yet another cream éclair into his extravagant and ever-open gob.

Apparently I am the son of my father.

Let it be known that if I have any children they will either be French or German . . . certainly not English! Even I refuse to be English: a silly race of island monkeys fit only for mowing their lawns and polishing the soles of their ridiculous and ostentatious shoes! Just so that you will be in no doubt, let me spell it out for you once and for all: I am not English. I am not a painter and what kind of idiot would want to be a poet or musician?

Poets and musicians, as is well known, are a bunch of vile, gaudy show-offs! And professionals are the sickest of the whole bunch! Firstly, I refuse to be a professional, and secondly, I refuse to be English!

I climb from my bed, dress myself and get out of this cardboard room and onto the fearful streets to see the pinched and frightened faces of the dead. I fill my pockets with monkey nuts and toilet roll from the bog across the landing and promise myself that one of these days I'm going to get a doodle on my arm, something ghoulish and unsettling, a real live tattoo to sit these half-wits on their stupid heels.

I walk up the alley, across New Road and up onto Jackson's Field. To get above this stinking town, to see the muddy swerve of the river, the dockyard and the Nuclear Submarine Base, Chatham Dockyard, below, then Rochester castle, the cathedral, the whole sickening panorama.

I sit down on the cold damp earth, pull half a packet of Weights from my pocket and immediately start practising my resistance to pain. I light one up and spit out the flakes of tobacco – real cigarettes don't have filters! I play with the smoke in my mouth, hating the taste of it, the tickling sensation that runs across the roof of my mouth. I cough it out, spit, then flip open my little bottle and take a swig of cheap whiskey.

For the purpose of actual tattooing, I will start drinking Woods Navy rum, 100%. The next bit of dough I come across, that's it – spent!

I place the burning cigarette up against the back of my left hand and stare into that singeing flesh. The pain rises sharply and I have to let out a little cry, my heart pounding, then slowly the intensity of the pain diminishes and a smell like burning hair fills my nostrils and my head goes light, like as if the top of my skull is being lifted off. After about a minute or so the cigarette goes out and I have to re-light it. I puff it back into life, place it back onto the little white patch of skin and slowly a blister rises up. I lift my hand to my mouth and taste it with the tip of my tongue . . . hot, hard and full of liquid. I puff the ciggy into a vicious eye then grind it out into the flesh, the blister bursts and cool water trickles down my hand and over my white knuckles.

I stand, throw the stub to the ground, and stare into the ice-wind. I put my hands under my armpits, squeeze my thighs together and rock pitifully, my eyes streaming.

One day people will honour me. They will crawl to me on their hands and knees, rest their heads on my lap like loving dogs . . . The wind will drop, the sun shine, the birds sing, and impossible butterflies will flutter in that beautiful spring air, their wings velvet-black, engraved with startling eyes the size of half crowns.

I sit on the kiddies' swings until I make myself feel sick, then meander around the field next to the fort til about half-three when the girls' school chucks out. I stand by the main gates and then head off amongst the buoyant crowd, flowing in and out between the bodies as they thread their way down towards the station, their shrill voices lift my angry spirits and I follow a group of four of them, each dressed in their silly matching navy blue uniforms. They dance like enchanting elves in front of me.

One of them, wearing bright red shoes and scarlet-red hair, drops her school satchel, bends down to pick it up and looks at me, her face upside down, framed in the crook of her arm. She stays like that for just a split second, her eyes studying me, then, laughing, she stands again and with a quick glance over her shoulder, runs on to catch up with her friends.

My eyes follow her dancing feet and suddenly I get it into my head that I must own one of those blood-red shoes, to hold it and caress it, to steal it from her dainty foot and kiss the little indentation where her child-like heel has stood. Yes, she must be the one! And I run to catch her up, intent on cutting in front of her and slyly taking a look at her pixyish face.

I quicken my pace and am soon abreast of her, running along in the gutter, my feet kicking great mountains of leaves to the left and right of me. I almost trip and fall in my desperation to know the outcome of this riddle.

As I draw alongside and pass her, I stare intently at her profile, my eyes dribbling over her brow and beautiful lips. She must feel the hunger in my look for she glances up and blushes.

The story that the scarlet-haired girl told her Indian friend whilst walking down Fort Pitt Hill:

There is a holy man, or sadhu, who lives in India and has kept his right arm raised completely above his head for the last twenty-two years as a penance, or as some sort of pathetic gift to God. Though the blood has long since drained from its finger tips and according to eye witnesses the arm now has the appearance of a rather dry and disgusting old twig, so that even God, in all his glory, would probably think nothing of slinging it straight onto the nearest dung heap.

Her girlish voice, which before had been high and trilling, suddenly grows hushed and I quickly look ahead, pull my hat down over my eyes, and run on towards the station, looking to my naked wrist, to make believe that I'm only running because I'm late for my train.

As soon as I get to the station, I turn and lean against the wall and watch them ambling slowly down the hill towards me. Her scarlet shoes and scarlet hair dancing in the sombre evening air. They cross by the roundabout and she sees me, turns to her friends and whispers something inaudible to my ears. The other girls look quickly at me, hold their child-like hands to their pink mouths and shriek with irritating laughter. As they draw closer still they grow silent again and stare down at the pavement. As they pass, I step out in front of them and address the scarlet-haired one.

'Excuse me miss, but apparently you find something amusing about me?' She looks at me in pure fear. 'It seems that for you I am a figure of fun.' I stare into her green, flint-like eyes and want to lick the lids; to kiss her and bite her wretched lips; to fall to the ground and lick the buckles of her scarlet shoes; to taste the cold bitter metal in my mouth.

She looks back at me agape.

'I address myself to the one I presume to be the ringleader of this sorry troupe?'

Dusk has already fallen and the taxi headlights glow like jewels behind her. The stench of exhaust fumes fills the air. No matter how hard I concentrate I can't stop my eyes from feasting on her feet. Waiting there for her answer I notice with pleasure that she has rather fat ankles and dimply red knees.

'Is it my face which amuses you the most? Or is it the fact that I am poor? Or perhaps it is because I don't dress fashionably that you torment me ... because, unlike you, I don't have such bright suggestful shoes? Or maybe you think that my whole body is somehow ugly and ridiculous?'

Quite why her violent red shoes intoxicate me so completely is beyond me. Why has God chosen this poor unfortunate girl for me to torment? All I know is that this special mixture of bewilderment and fear in her eyes excites me, and I have to use all of my self-control not to spit on her and bite her as we speak.

Just standing there in the same air that she breathes sends my blood raging. I put my hands in my pockets and feel myself. I must possess this scarlet-haired one, I must hold her and destroy her.

I stare down at her shoes again and become sure that I can hear little noises emanating from them, as their leather soles scuff lightly against the rough surface of the flag-stones.

At first I really had only been teasing her – just a mad fancy on my part, the brightness of her shoes catching my eye in that dreary afternoon – but now a genuine anger flares up inside of me, and I manage to convince myself that a great wrong has been done unto me by this sexual and spiteful girl.

I look up and down the street, tapping my foot as if impatient for her answer. I warm to my role.

Of course, the power of this girl-woman to humiliate me, terrifies me beyond endurance. After all, a young man stood next to a girl feels himself worth less than nothing. Everything that he needs and desires is held in the palm of her cool hand and the power is hers: whether to deny him, or to give him life itself. But now that I have boldly confronted her and grasped the nettle, so to speak, it is obvious that this so-called woman is nothing but a mere child and I, after all, am a man and must be obeyed at all costs.

Her nervousness excites me and I feel a ticklish spite crawl across the palm of my hand and I have to resist the impulse to slap her insolent thighs. I look again, long and hard, at those itching red shoes, then her white socks and silly chubby legs.

If it wasn't for this minor flaw I had discovered in her, if she had after all been quite impossibly beautiful, then I would never have had the heart to bully her so remorselessly. In fact, I would have wilted like a flower and crawled back into the gutter from whence I came. And again I feel my anger flaming in my chest; that such an ugly one as this, with her immense lard-like legs, should laugh in the face of a tortured young writer who is guilty of nothing more than minding his own business, nursing his tortured hand on a cold and bitter November afternoon . . . .

She stands there staring, I fancy, at the buttons of my shirt. Or perhaps at some ghastly imperfection of my throat. Her eyes wide like a startled foal . . . and my knees begin to shake. A sickening desire to turn and run headlong down into the bowels of the station overcomes me, but my legs will not respond. I'm just about to tell her that I am a sick and evil man and will throw myself under a passing taxi, when finally she opens her beautiful mouth and speaks. I watch transfixed as her tongue caresses the words inside her soft pink palate and pushes against her exquisite white teeth. Teeth that I could cry over, hold in the palm of my hand and treasure like pearls.

'We weren't laughing at you, sir, it was a joke. Jackie told us a joke, that's all.' Scarlet nods to Jackie.

I look down on a short, thick-set Indian girl stood obediently by her shoulder. Jackie looks up, nods her head like a Shetland pony and stares down at the gutter.

I look at the pair of them, my brain struggling for blood, and I am suddenly seized with indignation that they think me such a fool that they can fob me off with such a feeble excuse.

Was it possible after all that I had imagined the whole incident from start to finish? That they were never in fact laughing at me, but actually giggling at some pathetic schoolgirl joke?

'You have the audacity to laugh at me? You think I am physically funny? You should take a look at yourself my good girl, stood there with your ridiculously fat legs!' I spit it out and grin at her, looking to the other girls and nodding.

Scarlet's face takes on a bitten look and I have the sickening feeling that I have just reached over and crushed her heart in the palm of my hand like a dry leaf. Her teeth bite at her lips and a tear springs from her beautiful green eyes. The Indian girl reaches up and puts her arm protectively round Scarlet's shoulders and looks at me with eyes of burning hate.

'Come on, Kursty, let's go now. I'll walk home with you.'

She looks at me again, her eyes like black stones and she keeps them on me defiantly as she leads Scarlet away.

I am left standing there, my temples pounding. The way that girl looked back at me, I got the strangest notion that I was being cursed by a dark and malevolent witch. I console myself by reciting how pathetic girls are in their stupid gangs, locking away their beauty and keeping the favour of their naked bodies for their blond and stupid men, being too scared to ever stand alone. I convince myself that I've called their bluff and saved myself from a very tricky situation. They'll think twice before picking on some unfortunate young writer again!

I stick my hands in my pockets and cry out in pain as the back of my hand brushes against the coarse material of my pocket. Angrily I pull out my matches and cigarettes, light one up and stroll off round the back of the station.

I arrive on Maidstone Road, then quickly double back down the alley and running full tilt, arrive back at my starting place next to the taxi rank. I can just make out Scarlet's red hair and shoes as she turns the corner of Rochester Street. I take a last puff on my cigarette, throw it to the ground and head up after her.

Thursday:
I shall call her Kursty. She is a golden princess. I was walking between the bus stops between Walderslade and Chatham, saving precious coins, when I saw her walking with her friends outside the railway station.

Actually, I was giddy and in need of Aspros . . . She is divine and from heaven, an African princess, but white.

I teased her a little and I will have to destroy her friends.

Tomorrow I will dye my hair black.

When I get back to my bed-sit, I pull my suitcase from under the bed and spread all of my pornography magazines out across the stinking mattress. Just because a young writer is pursued and beaten like a hapless dog, it is no reason to kick him and deny him his rightful dinner. And if I am such a dog, and in many ways I have a heart like a dog, surely at least somebody out there will find it in their perfect human heart to pat me, rub my belly and even feed me a vile, stinking bone?

Women have such wonderfully hairy arseholes. If they're good enough for a dog to sniff at and breathe a lungful, then it's hardly surprising that I, as a young writer and dog myself, should gaze helplessly at some harmless photo of a poor woman with my heart in a state of near collapse. Because, after all, even mongrel dogs are allowed to dream sometimes and imagine themselves to be kings with all the bitches of the Doggy Kingdom coming running to them on heat with their tails held high.

I put my head on my pillow (my overcoat) and kiss it; it smells like an old blanket and I lean over and spit deliberately on the floor and smile gleefully to myself. After a short while I feel guilty and make myself get up and wipe it up off the dirty linoleum with the sleeve of my shirt.

In my latest photo-booth portraits, I can make out my new tribal scars and some broken boils. Shortly, I will destroy this epidemic of imperfections that dares to crawl across the face of a genius. I rip up the photographs one by one and drop them into my provisions box. Already, I have edited my collection down to fifteen.

I have decided to dedicate my poem to Kursty, and when it is published I will present her with a leather-bound copy outside Chatham Railway Station in honour of where we first met and bring to silence that bickering hoard of harpies that accompany her. I shall stand like a statue before her and my poems will fall like stones into her ice-cold heart and my princess will come running to me and fall into my open arms.

My favourite photograph of all shows me looking out into the world almost as arrogantly as my brother (which is no small achievement). Lately I have been taking close note of the play of my emotions and the beatings of my heart. I now know that I am better than him and that he must be destroyed. This is harsh of me, so I have decided that if he acknowledges me as the true gentle brother that I am, then I will embrace him and forgive him, which is the kingly way to behave in such matters.

In my next most favourite photograph my eyes are shut and I'm looking downwards as if I am about to cry. I have taken a long lug on my cigarette, held my breath in and my hair is just right; swept back and unkempt. 'It looks like a bird has nested in your hair!' my father used to bark at me, which I secretly loved. Anyone with an ounce of intellect can see that I'm a desperate man; that my heart is pounding from it; that I am feared and brave and a truly great young writer.

On second thoughts, I am so pleased with this new photograph that I now consider it my overall favourite bar none!

This evening I shall write a letter to my princess revealing my heart – the exquisite pain of love is something that all artists must endure, to be a young writer, after all, is to never be alone and a glowing rush of blood courses through my veins, knowing myself to be the living blood of all the greats – to destroy myself out of pure spite.

I roll onto my back and feel myself all over, chewing on my tongue with delight, then, springing to my feet, grasp the sink and stare into the shaving mirror.

'I will come for you tonight, Kursty, and you will be mine!'

I press my face roughly against the mirror, lick at the glass savagely and a sudden pain shoots through my nose. I run my fingers across my face feeling my chin and cheeks. Great dull boils are emerging from under my papery skin. Two previously undetected knots of pus form large painful masses in each nostril and my heart twists in agony upon itself. God save me! Oh, please save me! I want to be beautiful!

I fumble for my pencil box and snatch up my scalpel. I find three more heathen lumps in my chin and stab the blade into their centres, digging for that vile worm. I pull the cuts apart and mop at the pus with toilet paper, bursting the hearts out of them. I take up the blade again then feverishly move on and cut three small slits into my cheeks, just below the eyes, re-opening the old wounds, to see if I really do have blood – to see if I really can bleed.

'So, there is blood in your veins!' I speak. 'Or at least fake blood! Cheap theatrical blood! Silly orange blood. More like children's paint than blood!'

Standing there in front of the mirror, numb, the blood trickling down my chin and onto my naked breast ... And I look again to the mirror to see if I haven't really made the whole thing up from start to finish. I address myself to my image and make believe that I really am six years old and talking to my mother.

'What if I'm only dreaming, mummy? What if all of this doesn't really exist and I wake up in the morning and you're gone?'

I cross-question myself, determined to never come up with an answer that I can live with. Then I take my cock out and lean into the mirror, and I lose interest in my answer and I stare down at myself.

'This is for you Kursty, you whore! With all my sad heart!'

The blood really does drip from my chin.

I find her house number, walk up the pathetic garden path and peer in under the porch light to check that this really is the right one. The light is on but no one has seen me. I slip round the side of the house and take a look out back. All the windows there are in darkness except for the kitchen but you can't see in because of these net curtains ... I stand very still, waiting for about two minutes, my breath fogging at my mouth and the backs of my hands moon white, my cigarette wound showing like a sad black eye. There is no sign of life so I check round the garden and find this old shed ... I try the door, which is unlocked, step inside and feel around the walls in the darkness.

Actually, I bash my shin against something – against a ladder – and I'm positive that I'm bleeding. It's ghostly in here and I decide to get out before I knock something over or disturb the fat black spiders that are sure to live in here. What I find so hideously revolting about spiders is their vulnerability. The squashiness of their bloated bodies sickens me.

I adjust my rucksack on my shoulders and am just going to cut back round to the front of the house, when the top left-hand light goes on and I see Kursty walk naked across her bedroom. My heart kicks in, my head spinning with a million emotions. I put my hand in my pocket and feel myself, chewing on my tongue. She goes to her closet then walks back past the window again and the light clicks off.

Firstly, I want to run back and get the ladder from the shed, but another voice won't let me and instead makes me run back round to the front of the house and press the doorbell. I ring it six times and then bang on the knocker. I stand there listening to the sickening sound of my own heart. I try to halt it by breathing shallowly but then it forces into my throat and I have to gulp at the air like a drowned rat.

I am a desperate man with desperate hands. All the while my legs are telling me to turn and leg it screaming into the night. Then I see a shadow behind the door and somebody fumbling with the latch. The door opens a crack and the lady from the dole office peers out at me from behind her horn-rimmed spectacles.

'Yes?' she speaks.

There is the sound of a television set coming from the front room.

'I've come to see if Kursty's in.' I smile and stand back into the shadows. 'I wondered if she wants to come out for a picnic.'

She laughs thinly and then, lowering her head, looks at me suspiciously over her glasses.

'A picnic? At this hour?'

I turn around and show her my rucksack, tuck my thumbs under the shoulder straps and lift it off my shoulders.

'I've got some digestive biscuits and a bottle of lemonade, and two apples.' I turn back round and smile disarmingly at her. She narrows her eyes.

'What's wrong with your face?' she asks me.

I tuck my chin into my jacket.

'An accident,' I say quickly. 'I went through a car windscreen . . . Last week, up on the M2 bridge. A motorbike swerved to avoid a hedgehog and hit us straight on!'

She doesn't listen to a word and continues to study my face.

'Don't I know you from somewhere?'

I tell her that I can't think of anywhere, unless she used to be in the circus.

'Are you all right, Joyce? Who's there?' A man's voice comes from in the front room.

'It's a young man, he wants to see our Kursty,' she calls back.

'She's doing her homework!' he shouts. Which is a downright lie!

'He wants to know if she wants to go on a picnic.'

'Oh, bloody hell!' A little man comes through from the

front room, squeezes past an old upright piano and blinks at me.

'A picnic?' He pulls up his trousers just for the effect and folds his arms, stood there beside her.

'You go inside love, I'll handle this.' The lady from the dole office looks at me, sniffs, and disappears back into their strangely smelling hallway. She turns once more and I have to smile at her again. I try to see into their front room but she closes the door behind herself. The man raises his arm, leans across the door frame and pushes his glasses back onto his face. Actually, there's a fake set of horse brasses hanging in the hallway behind him, and the house smells of cauliflowers.

'If you want to speak to Kursty, you'll have to come back in the morning . . . At a reasonable hour . . . She's gone to bed.'

'But you just said she was studying her homework.' I smile at him, catching him out.

'In bed, studying her homework, what's the difference to you?'

'I'll just wait until she's finished,' I say. 'I'll wait for her out here, by the wall.' I turn and walk back up the garden path and sit myself down by the gate, next to the fir tree. The man carries on looking at me.

'There's no fur on this,' I call to him, 'you've been sold a fake!' I take off my rucksack and pull out my bottle of lemonade. I hold him with my eyes, unscrew the lid and, looking directly at him, take a long swig. The bubbles explode up my nose and I snort like a horse.

The little dad crosses his eyes and puffs out his cheeks then, apparently tiring of this pose, he tries standing around with his hands on his hips. I burp, screw the lid back on and stretch out full length on the wall.

'You'll have a long wait,' he shouts. 'You can sit there all bloody night for all I care!' and the door bangs closed behind him.

I sit up, look up and down the street and light a cigarette. I clean my fingernails with my pen knife. Twice I see the curtains in the front room twitch back and the face of the lady from the dole office peers out at me from behind the glass.

Half an hour passes, then I hear the front door go and the dad comes marching up the garden path, his mouth munching away on an imaginary pipe.

'Right, that's quite enough now! I think it's time you were off home son, don't you think? . . . Come along now, off with you! Off! Off! Off!' He draws up in front of me, his hands fluttering like moths in the night air. He even sticks out his chest at me, trying to exude an air of authority.

'You can stop all this nonsense right this second! I've asked you politely – now leave! Kursty is in bed . . . I don't know who you are or quite what you're up to, but this is a respectable neighbourhood and you're not lying about on my front wall like it's a rubbish tip!'

My left eye twitches and my bottom lip begins to tremble. To speak the truth I'm hurt by his hard and uncaring nature. Actually, inside I'm crying.

'Let me speak to Kursty.' I look at him, lick my lips and stare at the rose bush in next door's garden.

'You are leaving. Kursty has no idea who you even are!'

'She knows who I am!' I say with conviction, and look down and defy this dad of hers.

He takes a step back, the little muscles in his jaw release and tense. He pushes his glasses onto his nose again.

'She doesn't know you from Adam! She doesn't know who the hell you are! Do you understand me? Now if you don't get off my wall and clear off this second, I will be forced to call the police!'

Suddenly I start to cry. Great sobs well up from below my heart. I snatch at my breath, my chin trembling. And I'm seven years old, stood in front of Mister Clues, the Head Master of Lordswood Primary School, whilst he smashes me with his iron tongue, stamps over my young heart and destroys my dreams with glee, without so much as a drop of love within him.

I fall to my knees and rest my face against the harshness of the brick wall.

'You're lying,' I hiss. 'She loves me, I have the letters to prove it! You don't know, you don't know nothing! You're lying . . . Kursty loves me!'

His voice softens. 'Look, you're deluding yourself, son, Kursty already has a boyfriend . . . I understand, I really do . . . But don't you think that she's a little too young for someone of your age? She doesn't even want to speak to you.'

I twist my neck and stare wide-eyed at him. 'Liar!' I shout. 'You won't allow her to see me because you're keeping her for yourself, you disgusting old pervert!'

Inside I feel a little bit cheeky, almost as if I'm making myself angry on purpose.

He stares at me speechless.

'She asked me to come here!' I carry on, the story springing to my mind like a mad paper-trail which I feel somehow compelled to follow.

'She asked me to come here and steal her away from you in the middle of the night!'

'Rubbish!' he spits. 'What absolute rubbish, you're out of your mind. You . . . You . . .'

'Then how do I know that there is a ladder in the garden shed and that her bedroom is the top left room at the back? How would I know all that if she hadn't told me to come here and steal her?' I set my jaw at him triumphantly.

'Right, that's it! I've had enough of this bloody nonsense! I'm calling the police, you've had fair warning!'

He about turns and marches back up his path. He shouts it out into the night air. Actually, it was as if he wasn't addressing me at all, but had instead gotten it into his feeble mind to have a conversation with the rose bush that was growing next door. It occurs to me that he is going to reach out and rip it up by its innocent roots and then savagely stuff it into his pipe and start smoking on it. All in all the effect would have been so comical that I would have had to have laughed.

Once he gets to his front door he about turns and storms right up to me again jabbing me in the chest.

'Out! Out! Out! Get out! Joyce!' he shouts, 'Joyce!'

The front door opens and Joyce stands there in her dressing gown and fluffy pink slippers. She has taken her glasses off and removed her eyebrows.

'Joyce, call the police! I want to report a disturbance of the peace!'

He turns on me. 'I want you,' he jabs me again, 'off of my premises!'

'This isn't your road mister, you don't own the pavement.'

'Oh yes I do. Now off! Out of it!'

I stand back unable to believe his anger. I tell him that if my conversation has in any way alarmed or upset him, then I will apologise immediately.

'I realise that as Kursty's father it must be terribly hard for you, but it is hardly my fault that your daughter is a mature sexual being and has the normal healthy appetites of an animal.'

Just then, I see the curtains moving behind his shoulder and Kursty's face presses against the cold window-pane. I try to look away, to not draw attention, then she smiles at me and makes a little wave before stepping back into the shadows.

A radiant light surges through my entire being, filling my heart, as if a door that I hadn't even previously known existed, has been flung open and the full brightness of a spring morning burst in upon the blackness of my soul.

I look down on this ridiculous man stood raging in front of me and a sudden well of friendliness rises up from deep within me. The little dad glares up at me like an angry water beetle which, of all things, has found a heron standing knee deep in his pond and is busily eating up all of its fish.

He turns his head and yells up at the window. 'Go back to bed, Kursty! I will deal with you later!' He narrows his eyes behind his steamed-up glasses, his nose put on sideways, and I have to resist the urge to smirk.

'I'm sorry,' I say, 'it's just your nose . . . you look so serious.'
He turns and faces me again.

'Oh, but this is serious, young man! And I don't think you
know how serious! My daughter is fifteen years of age and I
am therefore still her legal guardian! If you choose to persist in
this ridiculous infatuation I will personally see to it that you go
to prison and will never ever set eyes on her again!'

'You can't do that,' I say, shaking my head.

'Oh, can't I? Well the police have already been called,' he
lifts his wrist watch and looks at it theatrically, 'and they
should be here any minute now!'

'But I love her,' I whisper.

'That's as may be, but she doesn't love you, does she? She
doesn't even know who the hell you are, for Christ sakes!' He
spits venomously, smelling victory and enjoying his sudden
surge of righteousness.

I look to him and back up to the empty window and I feel
something in my stomach give way and break inside me. But
beyond that I hope and build my dreams in fairyland,
somewhere where his viciousness cannot soil my heart.

I smile weakly at him and turn, the tears springing to my
eyes in hot jets. I hobble a few paces and my guts let go, my
pants filling with burning liquid.

'Don't forget your picnic!' he calls after me and shoves my
rucksack into my chest.

I make it down to the main road and the police car cruises me.
I glance timidly over my left shoulder to see if they make a U-
turn and they do. They do a little loop and I pull my hat down
over my eyes and try to walk on nonchalantly, as if I am merely
out on an evening stroll.

My chest aches of sobbing . . . the stinking liquid trickling
down my inside leg. I will outsmart these imbeciles in uniform.
I will show them what a first-class intellect is capable of in the
face of their repugnant chauvinism! Actually, they stop me
sharpish and peer at me with such disdain, as if to suggest that

I am nothing but a common criminal. There's two of them sat in there fiddling with their buttons. Both of them get out and the fat one leans me face down over the bonnet and starts rummaging through my pockets. He makes noises about my stink and, on the whole, says a lot of unkind things about me. But I fool them with my ring, which is in fact a water pistol. I know that I'm going to do it and I can't resist a little chuckle to myself. The one with the big blond face tells me that I should be careful not to get myself run over wandering the streets at this time of the night ... Actually, I was hoping that they might offer me a lift in their shiny new car. I pause a moment so as to give them the opportunity, but they just stare at my trick ring which the fat one holds in his fat, stupid fingers. He lifts it to his nose and sniffs. He squeezes the little bottle and some water spurts up and sprinkles into his left eye. He wrinkles his nose and dabs at it with his heavy serge cuff.

'It's a trick ring,' I explain to him as he glares at me, 'It's a water pistol.'

'So this was going to be your "little tipple"?' He holds me with his stern brows.

'Pardon officer?'

'Are you sure there's no drugs in it?' I grin at him.

'Yeah, I'm sure, officer. It came out of a Christmas cracker.'

He looks at me disbelieving.

'Well, all right then. But you watch it! Get yourself a torch, or wear something bright. We don't want to be scraping you up off the road along with the dog shit!' He drops my plastic ring into the centre of my palm. I look at their manly faces, but there's not a drop of love in them. Then they climb back in their car and speed off. I'm left standing there, stripped, half-naked, the wind howling between my ribs.

I have to hug myself and walk on, picking my way along the verge, the cars racing up behind, their headlamps leaping out of the darkness and startling me. I really am like a little red fox scurrying off to my god-forsaken den to sniff drugs out of my toy ring. Hee, hee, hee! And I have to chuckle to myself again at the naivety of our police force ... My heart twisting in my chest, huddled against the cold and the harsh adversity of life that seems to constantly seek me out and give me a good duffing.

I have had sex with a Jewish Lady who is the mother of two children, which is probably sinful, and my stomach hurts. She came and collected me in her car and then drove me back to my room the next morning.

When we arrived at her house she insisted that she wash my clothes for me, then ordered me to take a bath.

You have to cross her children's bedroom to go to the bathroom. I walked very quietly so as not to wake them up, but the Jewish Lady shouts at me that it isn't necessary as nothing on earth can wake them. To prove her point, she pulls the littlest one from his bunk and sleepwalks him out into the toilet.

'Now, you're not going to wet the bed are you, Mister Dis-Gus-tifer?!'

The little boy rubs his eyes and walks like a ghost. She yanks down his pajama bottoms and pulls on his little dinkle.

'Pee!' she orders and a little yellow jet splashes across the toilet seat. I have to pretend that I'm not really looking.

There are no seats in her house, you have to sit on cushions on the floor and pretend that that's normal. I sit cross-legged in her old dressing gown and arrange it about me so as to remain decent. The Jewish Lady stands, goes to the kitchen and returns with two bowls of food and some chopsticks. I look at it suspiciously and pick out the bits that I can eat.

Every time the Jewish Lady asks me a question, instead of listening to my answer, she raises her voice another pitch and shouts over me. And, if by chance I am allowed to finish my sentence, she immediately changes the subject, or utters some profound platitude or other in such a rhetorical way that you have to stare into your food, or feebly mumble 'yes' and feel like a complete and utter fraud.

The Jewish Lady is dark with a striking nose and chocolate-brown eyes.

Because of her kindness to me, I feel obliged to let her carry on abusing me in this manner.

'Why do you always run everywhere? You like running everywhere, don't you? Why did you dye your hair red?'

I really do try to answer her and just about get my tongue behind my teeth, when she suddenly jumps up, shouts out loud and throws another log onto the fire.

I stare into my bowl of gruel and chase a piece of grit round my mouth with my tongue. She finishes her meal and places her bowl down on the cork tiles in front of her, arranges her chopsticks and sits back. I watch her movements and do exactly the same.

'Why, you've hardly touched your food!'

'I ate all I could,' I apologize, 'It's my stomach, you see, I . . .'

She stares past me and enquires after my father's profession.

'He works in London, I think he . . .'

'Do you want to get rid of your spots? I've got a sunlamp, it's brilliant!' she screams.

'Does it work?' I ask hopefully.

She holds me with her chocolate eyes and her tongue comes out and licks at her soft lips.

'I think it's only natural after a good meal, to finish the evening in bed together, don't you?' she says in a throaty and sexual way. I look down into my half-eaten bowl of food and try to understand.

'Come on,' she teases, 'you don't want to have to spend the night alone in that cold depressing room of yours do you? You can stay here!'

She stands, walks across the room and picks up my jacket.

'I'll sew your buttons back on for you.'

'Thank you,' I say, and sit back and stare into the heat of the fire.

'Don't sit all the way over there.' She coos and pats the cushion beside her. I shuffle across on my buttocks. She takes my hand in hers and dangles a needle from the end of a piece of thread over the centre of my palm.

'If it makes a circle to the right you'll have a baby boy, and if it makes a circle to the left, it will be a girl.'

I watch the needle hanging in the air like lead. She rubs my palm with her thumb.

'Oh,' she says pointedly, 'you'll have none!'

I stare at the needle, willing it to twist in ecstasy.

'No!' she shouts with finality, 'definitely nothing! You'll have no children! It really does work; my midwife did it for me when I was pregnant with Dis-Gus-tifer. You'll have two beautiful bouncing boys, she told me.'

I shrug and draw my hand away.

Actually, I feel peeved that she should spring this undignified test of my manhood on me without any prior warning.

The Jewish Lady sits back dreamily, pleased as punch with herself, her chocolate eyes playing with me.

'Come on, let's go upstairs!' She pulls me to my feet and I follow meekly behind her.

I leave her at the landing and walk back across the children's bedroom and collect my vest and knickers from the dryer. I slip back into them, put some toothpaste on my finger, rub it round my bleeding gums, swill my mouth and spit. My poor face looks out at me from the mirror. I try smiling but it hurts my heart. Instead I grin my teeth ironically, turn the light out and pad back across the landing to her bedroom door. I walk in, lift the duvet and climb in on the far side. I lie there, my insides squirming inside me, my heart knocking like a knuckle on a plank. I hold my breath high in my lungs and listen out intently for her breathing. Presently, it grows shallower and shallower, until eventually she starts to snore gently, the air singing in her nostrils.

The darkness moves darkly around the head of the bed and I lie filled with the terrible fear that her children will find me here in the morning, in bed with their mother. And they will know that I am a bad man, only not a man at all, a man who will never bear children. And they will know that I am a boy, a mere pretender forcing myself on their poor hapless mother.

I doze intermittently, trying to force myself to sleep.

Sometime near morning something slithers beneath the sheets and rests warmly against my thigh; its fingers tug at the elastic of my knickers. I awake with a start and have no idea where I am. For five seconds I know myself as no one, and in those seconds my heartbeat fills the entire universe with dread. I open my eyes wide and stare into the blackness as that mysterious hand pulls and strokes at me.

Dread and lust course through my veins and brain, and I am nine years old, lying in bed with 'uncle' Norman, him tugging my trunks down round my knees and whispering – 'can you keep a secret?' – his hot breath on my child's neck.

A delicious sensation of being powerless and molested fights for possession of me. I shake my head in fear and can't allow that realisation to be. I stifle my cries in the certain knowledge that I am stained, filthy and bad.

She eases her hand inside my knickers and I hear a milk float trundling along the street beneath the window. The first light of dawn filters weakly into the room and she pulls on my thickening cock. Suddenly, she is upon me. She leaps into the saddle and slaps her hairy minge on my belly, her hair gone wild, filling my face. She pins down my arms, digs in her heels and rides like a cowboy, whooping and licking at my face. I lie there trapped, helpless beneath her, as she heaves herself up and down, grunting and smashing her pubic bone into the base of my cock. Fearful of failure, I concentrate and try to remain a man.

She bounces on her bony arse and pushes my face into her fried egg tits. I wriggle to be free ... a terrible vision of her great hairy cunt giving birth to her two sons on my lap fills my mind and I gag with disgust.

She tries to kiss me, her tongue snaking at my lips and weakly I respond to her, excited but repulsed, her mouth tasting of old leather. Then, filled with shame and self-loathing, I roll over and bury my face into the pillow.

At five-thirty her children come into the bedroom. I hear their padding feet and little voices.

'This is Robin and this is Gus.' She introduces them.

I peer out boyishly from under the covers. The two sprogs stood at the foot of the bed staring at this strange evil man lying in their mother's bed.

'Hello,' I say weakly.

The eldest one lifts the corner of the cover and peeks underneath. I snatch at it, anger rising hopelessly in my throat ... the fear that they will see my nakedness.

'He hasn't got anything on, mum!' he shouts in wonder, and both of them shriek and try to climb in under the covers with me, and my heart feels smaller than anyone else's in the whole world.

Wednesday:
A gale is blowing today and the whole street has taken on the look of an old blurred photograph. I saw my elder brother on Chatham High Street, which was quite comical as he believes himself to be 'Of The City of London'.

He has sold two of his paintings and bought himself a

special 'artist's' shirt. He opened his jacket and showed it to me, but I purposely kept a cynical sneer playing around my lips and stared off into the far distance, all the while jangling some loose coppers noisily in my pocket. He looked at me sideways and told me that I was a provincial and a coward and that I don't know how to take good advice, which is correct.

'You always have to pretend that you know it all, don't you!' he yells at me, trying to make me look him in the face, which I do. I turn and hold his dark eyes with my own. He brings his fingers up and starts rummaging around in his eye bags, his nails tearing away at the flesh, obviously fearful of my penetrating gaze and the fact that I can see everything.

He looks away at an interesting spectacle in the gutter and then fixes me again with his angry eyes.

'We've all been there, sonny! I was just like you a few years ago, but now I've changed! I'm older and wiser! I've got more experience than you!' he jabs me in the chest with one of his thick fingers, 'and I've read more books than you!'

And then he just turns and walks away. I watch him saunter off into the distance.

'You should try following the example of The Buddha!' he shouts into the wind, his fingers clutching at his arse.

I smile after him, willing him to walk under a passing bus, if you must know.

In the afternoon I also saw the Jewish Lady. She came into the cafe where I have my food. She sat down at the same table and she held me with her chocolate eyes and told the whole room that I was useless in bed. I stared down at my hands, my chest became unbearably tight and a dancing pain reached out into the distant extremities of my body.

Deep down I still smart from every slap I've ever received, from every hurt done unto me because, no matter what type of brave face we may put on, some things stay with us for ever. My mother, for one, sits like a fat goose in her armchair, trying to hatch an old egg, forever mulling over all the injustices that she perceives as having been done unto her by the world and my father. Firstly planning her revenge, then apologising on his behalf. Hating him, then damning herself for her own inadequacies. In short – re-living every slight over and over again in her own peevish mind.

At precisely five o'clock this evening I followed my princess home from school, her scarlet shoes dancing before me.

I have my penknife in my pocket and have cut a length of rope from which I have fashioned myself a handsome belt . . . I have acne, a chronic headache and some special spot cream.

Somebody has put these blind boils in my face and they will have to pay! There's absolutely nothing you can do to burst the pus out of those fellows, the only way is to cut into them with a razor, pull the skin apart 'n' mop up the blood with toilet tissue, then you can fish out the little knots of pus from in amongst the sticky blood.

Murder, in some ways, might be amusing, but killing small children is beyond a joke. Of course, there is nothing actually funny about death or ghosts and children's ghosts, I should imagine, are far more frightening than their grown-up counterparts. Especially the ghosts of murdered children.

I have taken a new portrait of myself in the photo-booth at The Pentagon Shopping Centre, with my hair greased back, and wearing a blackened old suit. I look like Ian Brady, which is contentious and exciting.

Some people will say that my mind is running completely out of control, which it is, but that isn't true. Because, no matter which way you look at it, the mind doesn't like to be studied and makes a complete mockery of a young writer's honest attempts to follow it, to be friends with it, and to understand its feverish and unnatural desires.

In my dream Kursty wants for me to stay with her the whole night.

I walk her home from school and I can stare at her scarlet hair and dancing red shoes as much as I please.

Now, in the daylight, I can see that what had appeared to be a garden is in fact a crumbling front yard. And rather than living in a salubrious middle-class neighbourhood, Kursty's family actually inhabit nothing but a wretched hovel on a council estate. So they are poor after all, and what I took to be an emblem of power and privilege has turned out to be nothing but a trick of the moonlight.

On her doorstep I hand her my little love note and look at the pale freckles on her sexual upper lip and she blushes. My heart thumps in my mouth and she drags me into the hallway, holds me by the collar and stares into my eyes. She then turns and leads me upstairs by the hand.

Her parents aren't home from work yet; that's about the long and the short of it. The house still smells of cauliflowers and the wallpaper is brown and orange. Then she shows me her room, a landslide of crap, her bed emerging like the prow of a ship from out of the avalanche. My pretty little lunatic picks her way across the bomb site, her little arse jutting out behind her, encouraging me to follow it.

The whole set-up has me scratching my head the minute I walk in there. A regular bedlam in miniature ... And her showing me her room like that, before I even have a chance to give her my little letter, my declaration of love ... I'd sweated over that masterpiece all night. I'd dotted all the 'i's perfectly. She tosses it onto her dresser and gives me a squeeze ... I see it slipping down behind the mirror, my sonnet of misgivings, my heart bared.

She takes a real long slug on her hip flask and offers me a swig, just a nip, mind – gunpowder! Kursty's addicted to cheap vermouth mixed with cider. That's her little tipple, her hobo's cocktail. I sit there watching her grinning at the label.

'Navy rum!' she tells me. 'My grandmother brews it herself in Budapest.' And then she knocks it back in two glugs, wipes her mouth with the back of her hand and leaps on me, holds me down and licks me all over like a hound. I prop myself up on my elbows.

'I can't stay for long,' I tell her. 'I just dropped by to hand you my letter.'

And she smiles, and her tongue comes out and licks at her lips. 'Oh, but you can't go yet, you haven't even had a drink!' She tells me to stay put whilst she goes downstairs and lifts a bottle from her old man's drinks cabinet. I have to wait there examining the lumps in my face with my dirty fingers, then she comes back in with a half bottle of scotch, empties it into a glass and hands me it.

I take a swig, sit on the bed and look at the carpet. Kursty meows at me and comes across the floor on all fours. I look up and nearly spill my drink. I back-track, scampering amongst the duvets ... Then she pounces, gets me in a clinch and blows hot air up my nose. My arms are trapped behind me, supporting our combined weight. She giggles and simpers, licks my eyelashes ... Bites my tongue and doesn't come up for air. I'm left at her mercy. She paws at me and shakes me between her teeth ... Gives me another nip of scotch and drags me under the covers.

Kursty is worried by the idea of me pushing my thing inside her and she doesn't like me licking her arse, which is like a star of god. I ask her if I can fuck her in the arse, but she says that it is unnatural, and that her school psychiatrist says it is actually illegal. Which is a stupid thing to say.

If Kursty were to try and stop me from reading my mens' magazines, I would have to smash her, this girl who I have given the power of life and death over me.

I lie in her arms and she breastfeeds me and I feel like a powerless little titty-boy whose mother is going to leave him soon. I will soil her and degrade her and look for any excuse to make her sorry, to make her apologise for all the past wrongs done unto me by the race of woman, so help me God! Because I know that in the end, no matter what depths I sink to and how much I crawl, Kursty will smash me and take the favour of her body with her, and thereby prove that I am unlovable. And then people on the street will be able to point at me and say, 'there goes a man who can't keep hold of a schoolgirl, let alone a real woman! She left him to find a better man, a man with more cock, more spunk and greater under-standing!' And I shall be shamed and stand there wanking into the darkness as she runs smiling into the arms of her shiny new man.

Her name is Kursty and it will always be Kursty. And her name means everything to me and it will always mean every-thing to me. And I love her out of sheer gratitude. That she could kiss and hold one as low and as ugly as me, and allow me to press my foul stinking body into hers, to allow me to kiss and lick her; and for her youth and beauty; and for her fearlessness in not being afraid to walk the streets by my side and show this vile hiccupping world just what sort of beauty I am capable of possessing. And so I bow down to God in thankfulness for this miracle: that such a woman could love me, which I don't believe and will never believe, and I will break her so-called love just for the sheer hell of it – to call her bluff and prove that it never really did exist at all, and I will smile at her tear-stained face and trembling lips and hate myself for it.

I have been sitting in this wardrobe for four hours now, my knees jammed into my chest. Ever since Kursty's mother returned home unannounced at six o'clock, let herself in the front door and squawked 'hello!' in that guttural tongue of hers. Kursty leaps from the bed and stalls her at the top of the stairs. There's no doubt that the old bat is intent on getting into this bedroom and smelling the sheets for the scent of men. Kursty sweet-talks her whilst I slide quietly from the bed, gather my clothes together and climb in here to squat on a pile of her rotting shoes. I pull the curtain behind me and peek through: a mound of dirty washing heaped up against the bed; a used cup and plate; the spunk rag – full of my spunk – a bit of the windowsill and a strip of orange and brown floral wallpaper.

Kursty says that I am full of spunk and wants to know if I could fit my balls into her as well, which is impossible.

'I like the way you keep your legs open wide when you fuck me. Tom never used to do that.' And I feel my cock fattening up just to hear her say it, which is rude and indecent.

I pull out one of her scarlet shoes from under me, sniff at its insides, then kiss it, turn it over and lick the sole. It tastes of grit and I have to clean my tongue on the curtain. Indistinct voices come up through the floor from the kitchen below, but I can't understand anything of what's being said. Kursty's voice sounds like a plane going over and her mother sounds like an old dog having a fight with a dirty rag.

My left calf is cramping up so I let it poke out from under the curtain and then I hear them come out of the kitchen into the hallway. If Kursty comes in here I will force her onto the bed and fill her with spunk again in front of her mother, and the old dear will applaud as it pumps out of me and into her precious daughter. I wonder if there really is a chance of having sex again, which I feel compelled to do.

I stick my head out and the alarm clock clicks: 9:42. Kursty is the answer to all of my dreams and will soon leave me, which I shall never allow her to do.

I reach out through the curtains and grab a pair of her dirty knickers up off the floor. Kursty's piss flaps are so plump and hairless that I call them bomb doors. There is this white gunky stuff in the crotch of her knickers which doesn't come from me and smells bad. I put the gusset to my mouth and force myself to taste it with the tip of my tongue, which makes me retch.

'Oh Kursty, I'm loyal in my own way, ever-so loyal. That's what's sad. It doesn't last, once you lose your heart it gets harder and harder to ever find it again. But I offer it up to you Kursty – my love, a token, something to be held and cherished, not dropped and stepped on like a black slug. So hold me forever, Kursty, so that the world can never harm me or hurt me. But I will never speak of this and if you cannot guess of my need then I will hate you for it forever.'

What I like best is that she's been in the nut house, and one day soon I'm going to have to go there because I'm unstable.

Today, I will leave this town and never speak to Kursty again. I tell you, a whole month of losing myself in love and goo. Well, I have shown her my colours and now I shall walk on. Argh! My little sweetheart, don't play games with me. My name is Loveday, William Loveday, judging by my initials, and you'll do as well not to forget it!

Her name is Kursty and it means everything to me. Her name is Kursty Morgan and it means nothing to me. Her name is Kursty and I will destroy her before she destroys me.

My brother's girlfriend is an Indian doctor called Meena, who has kissed me, though I have declined to have sex with her.

All the little intimacies I held for you, Kursty, I shall deny and destroy. I shall deny categorically that I have ever known a Kursty Morgan and lie in the face of God. If we pass on the street, I shall secretly smile, for I have been first in many ways and have put my tongue in your most secret place. And no matter what you may believe, I will always hold one fragile part of you, Kursty, and can take it out and smash it anytime that I so choose!

Kursty, take me back, let me smile in your mouth. Let me suck on your pink tongue and wank myself into your dress. I throw up this matter of my heart in your face, Kursty. I can't let go. I have nothing to give, and stare with bankrupt eyes. But I will not deny myself, Kursty, I will point the finger and betray all of your confidences! I walk in these streets, in these bars, but next morning I awake alone and you aren't there, Kursty. Though I hold you in my guts, and lick this sour mattress, grieving with these stinging tears. How is it possible, Kursty, to show you the depths of my love? You who hold that power over me and smash it like porcelain despised. I will not give away my gifts so easily again, Kursty, and will instead avenge myself against the race of women, soiling them and degrading them, looking for any excuse to make them sorry. Until you crawl to me upon your bloodied knees and worship before me, Kursty, licking at my hanging cock and apologising for all the past wrongs which have been done unto me (which is wrong of me I know, Kursty, and I ask you to please, if you can, forgive me). Above all else I love you, Kursty, because you are the one who smashed me and gave me the pasting that I so richly deserve. The one with the courage to stand up and push me away. To laugh at my vile blubbering mug and kick me! And, like a mother standing, you tuck away your milk-heavy breasts and leave, thereby starving this helpless infant, and so I crawl on the floor before you, Kursty, in worship, my princess, in awe of your power and coldness.

Friday afternoon:
I lean into the wind and battle my way down Military Road. I cross at The Brook, walk into the Drill Hall and enquire whether my dole check is ready, which it isn't. I pull my hat well down over my eyes in case Kursty's mother is working behind the desk, but she isn't. The man behind the counter looks at me mockingly and asks me a lot of impertinent questions about my names and whether I am really looking for work at all, which I'm not.

I push out of the building and run straight across the road, dodging between the traffic in a manner that my mother told me never to do. A strange light-headedness takes hold of me and I feel positive that I am about to see Kursty and her mother getting out of a sky-blue Volkswagen and walking hand in hand into Millets to buy Kursty a rain hat.

I stand outside The Pentagon Shopping Centre waiting for them to appear. Something that people shouldn't laugh at is watching a lot of silly shoppers crawling up and down the High Street, their faces ravaged with delight and misery, the wind so strong that they are forced to lower their bodies and cling to the pavement like a lot of silly insects. Shopping in this manner is something that you shall never see me doing. I force myself to look away, which means I will probably miss seeing Kursty and her ridiculous mother. If indeed they do choose this particular hour to come shopping for rain hats.

Next, I see a flash and something hits me in the eye. I turn and stagger against the wall, my head thundering like a freight train and I go down. My hands dance like white skeletons before me, the blood drained from my skin like as if someone had opened my wrists. One second I'm standing there, holding my hat on against the breeze, the next I'm knocked sideways and no little pill can straighten me out. Full-blown, flashing lights, like a punch up the bracket. The world slides away from me . . . Toothache of the eye socket, just up and behind it, my left eye . . . I hold onto it . . . My knees shaking . . . I can't stand . . . I have to go down . . . to get my head level with the pavement . . . dull, a million patterns . . . rhythms of the blood . . . I have to hit the deck, to hold on . . . to grin and bear it . . . I crawl the length of the High Street, dragging myself to my home, through my doorway . . . up to my bed . . .

I blink through the pain, ever present. Three, four days, then a week . . . ticking . . . I wake to it every morning . . . I mustn't jerk my head, no sudden movements. It powers through my brain like a throbbing current. It recedes, it comes back, it reaches new crescendos. It goes to sleep with me and wakes up with me in the morning. I bite at the pillow and whinny like a horse – a gentle, joyful neigh.

A week passes and finally it's on the wane. I shake my head like a block of cheese. That's how I can tell if it's still there. I take my jaw in one hand and the top of my dome in the other and twist . . . Little cracking noises . . . I force it – snap! I begin to feel better, no more fairy lights . . . The noise dies away . . . Just a few murmurs . . . A dullness, but distant. I'm over the worst, my head becomes my own again . . . hollow . . . Puffing on ciggies, my hand lifts up and my lips pout. I take a drag, a horrible lungful ... And the head ... the ache still there, not quite past, waiting, like a sentinel.

These headaches of mine date from when I was a kid, nine or ten years old. Starting up every tea-time, after school: dizzy spells. My mother gave me Aspros in threes, they clog up your throat ... powdery ... I went bug-eyed.

'Swallow them!' she ordered. They go down, then they come back up again, they re-emerge. I spat chalk.

'Don't drink and don't smoke,' the quack tells me. 'It's bad for your health.'

I nod, oh yes, I know ... He's telling me nothing new ... Really? It's bad for me? Well, I can't say that I haven't been told. Forewarned, so to speak.

'But if I committed suicide wouldn't that be bad for me as well?' I ask him cheekily.

And he sits there fiddling with his stethoscope.

'How are your bowels?' He looks sternly into my eyes, and I look away, out of his window and into the car park and the housing estate beyond. There is an old lady with her face painted white climbing through his rose garden.

'These days we have painkillers that can vastly reduce the discomfort,' he pipes up again, 'they can be very effective.'

The lady is now directly outside his window and starts to claw on the glass with her black-painted fingernails.

'How long will I have to take them for?' I ask him.

'If you continue to suffer from migraines, then for the rest of your life.' He stands and lets the blind down.

'How do you know that it's not a tumour?' I sit there, cross my arms and legs and stare at him. I'm boring him but I refuse to budge. Finally, he stands, comes out from behind his desk.

'OK, stand up ... touch your nose ... close your left eye ... now the other hand ... close your right eye ... Aah, yes!' he checks his onion, 'just as I thought, nothing!'

'No tumours?'

'I honestly don't think so . . . we'll have to wait and see . . . take these pills and if there's no change for the better then come and see me again in a couple of weeks . . . A tumour? Probably not. At least, not by my reckoning . . . Nothing to worry yourself about, anyroad . . . You'll just have to learn to live with them . . . The headaches.' He looks at me thoughtfully. 'I can give you a month's supply of pain killers; that will be enough for you to be getting along with, for the time being, won't it?'

If you want to know my opinion, doctors are a bunch of evil do-gooders in the pay of the devil and the pharmaceutical industry.

I pout and stare at the carpet. Some people think that I'm sulky by nature. Him and his 'I don't think so'. Right, I'll be on my way then. 'Maybe, maybe not.' His big opinion? My tumour? He consults the stars and shakes his head. The wind tells him no. I walk out and leave. Me, who's so polite that it's painful. I apologise for wasting his time, see myself to the door and bow deeply.

Doctors really are the pits. That useless quack can't get rid of me quick enough. All he wants is to see my arse disappearing out of his surgery door pronto, so's he can get a real live paying patient up on his table. Hard cash or drop dead! That's the new medical ethic.

I pick myself up and button my collar. Painkillers? No thank you, doctor, I have my own supply of Aspros. My mother sends them to me in bulk. They taste of chalk, don't you know? And are apparently very good for the heart. Me and my brain tumour make our excuses and leave. We will have to nurse ourselves, because it's obvious that this quack couldn't give tuppence if I drop down dead in the street, just so long as it isn't in his surgery hours.

The daylight hits me and I wobble. I grasp hold of the railings and hug them to my heart. I've got to get down onto the ground, to feel my temple against the cool pavement. I can't stand heights. I spread my arms and feel my cheek against the damp bricks. We need love and I kiss them.

I twist in my sleep; I hold onto the bedposts and sing ... The lights die down and I lie bathed in sweat ... I chew on my tongue and taste blood, I have a toad in my mouth ... I wake myself up ... That's what I must have been doing ... Lying here, munching away on my tongue and tasting the pain.

I open my eyes, playing peek-a-boo-narrow slits – I wince and cringe, waiting for the blow to my head. I roll my eyes back and forth in their sockets and press my eyeballs with my thumb and let out a little squeak. To feel the pain, to take a peek at the ache from the inside: that's where it lives – burrowed back in there like an earwig. Down on the left side, a few inches back, lodged between the cheek and the brow. The type of thing that shouldn't be allowed. One of God's dirty little tricks.

I've been lying here for two whole solid days now and no one's even bothered to look me up, even bothered to check if I'm dead. You don't get many tears shed on account of a slight headache, it doesn't even register on the sympathy scales. And you can't explain it to anyone. They want to see the scars, the blood and the pus, the whole horror show. They're happy to know you're suffering, but where's the blood?

I lie there on my back staring up at the ceiling. There is a damp patch and a little drip forms there every two minutes or so; it plinks to the floor just next to the empty wardrobe.

Actually, my landlady did come into my room this morning, without knocking, and insolently told me that I shouldn't be lying about in bed all day, but should get up, get on my bike, find a job and pay her last month's rent!

'You've got a headache? Headaches! Humph! That's nothing, just take a look at this!' And she pulls up her slip and shows me a big raggedy scar that runs from one side of her disgusting belly to the other.

'There's thirty two stitches in that! That's from when I had my Raymond!' She adjusts herself, tucking her vest back into her flesh-coloured tights. 'I lost five pints of blood. The doctor said I was bleeding like a stuck pig! And it was black as ink and really thick! Have I shown you my veins? Look at this! They had to peel this one out, it swelled up like an aubergine!'

Me and my pathetic headache can go take a running jump! Go sing it to the birds kid, go on, clear off, cock sucker!

But I tell you in all sincerity, with no frills attached and joking apart, they haven't invented the pill that will measure up to one of these monsters: deadening, constant, repetitive ... A Blitz! ... Five days. Aspros? I've taken so many Aspros that I'm pooing powder. And all the colours, like Smarties. Only a joke, in poor taste I admit, but forgive me, if you can, my little indiscretions.

I lie back and squint through the pain, my overcoat jammed under my neck in a hard knot.

I have been to see a female herbalist, who tells me that I should not eat chocolate or cheese, and that if I don't stop drinking whisky it is going to kill me!

'What if I commit suicide?' I asked her, which is my special answer, and she looked at me from under her glasses.

My mind is swimming with a million silly thoughts and fears ... Actually I'm dreaming ... But no matter how toughly I cross-question myself I can't find one reasonable excuse for my miserable state of mind and sickening paranoia. Whatever honourable reason I come up with I immediately hold it up for fresh ridicule and mercilessly pull it to bits in front of my own eyes.

I still have a headache and woke up at least three times during the night.

I have to go to the window, lift the sash and take a piss down into the dark and mysterious yard below. The sound of my sprinkling comes back up to me and I get a sickening feeling that a large wolf, or bat, is about to smash through the window and devour my chest. I scamper back to my bed and lie there trying to stop breathing.

Around four o'clock, I hear a police siren out on the main street and have the most terrible vision of the police smashing down the front door, mounting the stairs and dragging me from my bed for some heinous crime which I have unknowingly committed. Namely, the murder of a small bird-like girl-child who I chased unswervingly through my vicious dreams. The girl now lies dead, her limp pale body concealed in my blue cardboard guitar case which leans slumped against the chimney breast. Such a silly tiled hearth with its empty and useless grate, like a set of busted black teeth.

No matter how viciously I throw myself about on that stinking mattress, I still can't fall back to sleep and an ice-cold night sweat streams off my flanks, chilling my body and making the sleeping bag quite wet. Try as I might, my mind runs on thinking and thinking regardless of what I desire of it. In fact, it seems to me that my thoughts not only ignore me but actually go out of their way to defy me and do the exact opposite of my wishes, purely out of spite, and then to just sit there gloating like a bunch of smug, puffed-up devils.

I unzip and step out onto the cold linoleum floor. The sweat freezes on my body and I have to rub myself quite vigorously with the moth-eaten blanket. One of these days my brother will ask for his sleeping bag back. He will demand it and say that he has owned it from day one, from when he was a boy scout, in fact. And then he will also demand the return of his red leatherette guitar in its blue cardboard case and the remains of his pornography collection and then I will be finally finished, I will own nothing, and I can quietly disappear.

I climb back into the wet sleeping bag and kick my feet about, trying to generate some warmth. I race them up and down on the spot, ripping still further the nylon quilting, which gives me a quiet satisfaction. I count to one hundred then lie there motionless listening to my rasping breath. I honestly want to fall asleep again but just can't manage it. My ears follow every creak in that haunted house, my head boiling with a million disconnected thoughts. Outside, I can hear the low moan of the milk float doing its morning rounds.

I wake up again about ten and I've got this stinking cold; my mouth full of snot and my head clanging. I am hungry. 'Hunger is a good thing', I tell myself, 'for one it sharpens the mind and secondly it removes fat.'

Today I will eat nothing, except maybe a handful of monkey nuts and possibly a bar of chocolate. I reach over for my jacket hanging on the bedpost, and pull a pack of aspirin from the pocket. I swallow six. They taste like sweet chalk. They are good for the heart, I tell myself.

Every morning now I examine my headache when I first awake. Feeling it building stronger and stronger until about four in the afternoon when finally it cripples me and I have to go down onto the floor and beg for mercy, chewing at the loose strands of carpet. Only in the evening when I get drunk is there any peace for my poor head. I have decided to stop eating cheese.

Masturbation, in my opinion, is a fine pastime. Not only does it offer excellent exercise, but it also relieves a build up of excess pressure – although the Chinese tell us that it depletes the life force and is therefore just another form of suicide.

I wipe myself on the blanket and suddenly a sentence runs across my mind, quickly followed by a second. I pull at my jacket and purposely rip the pocket in my rush to get my notebook free. I grab my biro and scribble furiously, trying to keep up with the mad torrent of thoughts that spill like hot blood across the page. Words pile up on top of words, yet others shout at me to take notice of them, and together they jostle over the page, ill-formed, illogical and mis-spelled. A great vomit of half-formed consciousness.

I hold the pages in my hands and kiss them, I can't believe my eyes, a miracle of God! Every word a gift from some magical unknown place. I gurgle with glee, spittle drooling from my lips. My fingers cramped, knotted to my pencil in a fit, feverishly trying to keep up with the pictures that crash against the insides of my skull in great waves. Suddenly the vision of a great epic opens up before me. The story of a man who is a man, but then again is not a man. A man ostracised by his own people for daring to show them the blackness of his own soul. A man who is then savagely sacrificed to an evil and unforgiving God. A zombie man. A mummified man who returns from the dead to haunt their dreams and nightmares. A man who is not a man, but then again is a man, a man who has been shrunken by the meanness of the world. A man who would love, if he were in turn loved, but who, in desperation, collects children's shoes.

The skin of my temples sings with ecstasy as I feel myself at the helm of this wonderful work. I write like a demon, filling page after page of my notebook – my special author's notebook – the pencil scouring into the paper with such force that the words are engraved clear through to the next three pages.

After two hours or so, the torrent begins to stem and I can think more clearly to write down the story that is unfolding from above. By mid-afternoon I have filled my notebook and the backs of twenty or so of my drawings. My left shoulder aches through resting my weight upon it and the snot has formed a thick yellow crust on my upper lip. I pick at it, see blood, and go into a sneezing fit.

The linoleum is icy cold and outside it has been snowing slightly. The cistern in the downstairs bog is completely frozen and held in a block of ice. I sit and piss and refuse to allow myself to shit. Instead, I stand and I tell myself that I have to shit on the floor, which I do. I then order myself to pick it up and place it, by hand, into the lavatory bowl. I automatically do as I'm told. I squat down on the floor and defecate. I turn and check the mess. A little spurt of pee has gone down my trouser leg. I bend down, scoop up my poo and make myself sniff it, putting my nose right up against it. Steam rises and a lovely warm stench. I make myself hold it for twenty seconds, then I drop it fearfully into the pan. As a reward I allow myself to wash my hands in the kitchen sink. In fact I tell myself off in no uncertain terms and scrub my nails viciously with the scrubbing brush, until my cuticles start to bleed. Then, I have to put my fingers in my mouth and taste that there is no shit left under my nails. I bite at them and tear off little chunks of nail, then force myself to swallow them. I bow humbly to myself in the mirror, thank myself for this delicious meal and only then do I allow myself to go out, although I don't let myself button my jacket as a punishment, which is cruel of me in that icy wind.

Monday:
Sullenly, I walk the street, my feet kicking out in front of me like a pair of old rags, the sole of my left shoe flapping like a sad mouth. Lately, all of my energy seems to seep out of me the minute I climb from my bed and it takes every last ounce of effort just to stamp my feet into my sad shoes and shuffle towards the door.

There's no doubt that the spring has gone completely out of my step. I let my hands dangle in my pockets, stick my tongue in my jaw and slouch along the high street like a knackered dog.

Dully, I become aware that I have been stroking a large lump in my left groin for the last half hour. I stand stock still and toy with it with my thumb and forefinger. My heart pounds in my temples and dark thoughts of death invade me – cancer! The lump sticks out just at the point where my left leg joins onto my torso. I run my fingertips feverishly over it and then press it spitefully and yelp. I call myself a fool, a fool and an inter-fering old hag!

As I stand there, imagining all manner of hideous endings for myself, the street grows hushed and becomes menacingly quiet. The usual non-stop flow of traffic seems to have petered-out into nothing and life come to a complete and utter stop. All that remains of the normal hustle and bustle is one lone corpo-ration bus disappearing into the icy fog, its rear lights showing miserably in the distance. Then a man appears and starts to totter along the road towards me, a pair of scruffy dogs tugging him on their strings. As he comes nearer I notice that he drags one leg behind him and seems to be carrying on a conversation with himself . . . his tongue licking feverishly at his parched lips . . . and apparently giving himself a thorough bollocking. He draws to a halt beneath a lamp post and his mutts both look up at him as if to ask what type of idiot he is. Choosing to ignore their impudence their master stands swaying slightly in an imaginary breeze, apparently poised to cross the street. He looks both to the left and to the right with his bullet head, then changes his mind and sets off with his rat-like dogs towards the next lamp post. I re-feel the lump in my groin and when I next look up, the man is disappearing from view behind an old, peeling hoarding. Large irregular bushes raise up their unkempt arms and welcome him into their midst. In short, both him and his wretched dogs are swallowed whole by the dense, fog-bound undergrowth. It seemed at that moment as if the street breathed out a deep and painful sigh, and I got the distinct impression that I was the last person who would ever again have to look upon this sorry spectacle with its peculiar sombreness and dismal shop fronts.

Suddenly, I order myself to jump in under a doorway as I have the unpleasant notion that something very large and heavy is about to drop from out of the skies and smash me. I peer fearfully out into the fog. There's a loud grinding of gears and a petrol truck comes lumbering out of the mist and the endless flow of traffic resumes. The man with his two dogs sticks his bloodshot head out from behind the hoarding and surveys the street with his roving eyes. Likewise, his dogs stick out their shabby muzzles, pulling ahead, apparently intent on dragging him under the wheels of the passing truck. The leading dog sniffs the air and, barking gleefully, leans its weight against its lead. Just as it seems that disaster is inevitable, the master swings the vicious and disobedient mutt round on its string, curses its life and stumbles across the quite uneven paving slabs towards me. I turn, desperately looking for escape. I realise that I am standing in the entrance of the Rose and Crown public house. I back into the double doors behind me and almost fall arse-first into this smoke-filled cavern. Loud, uncouth voices rise up to me and somewhere, off in the distance, a man shouts at me to 'close the fucking door!' which I actually already have.

My eyes smart from the acrid smoke. I turn and trip on the lower step, almost hurting my ankle. Just then the door crashes open behind me and there stands the bullet-headed man with his two mutts. His forehead glistens in the dirty yellow light, and he swings his head around the room as if searching out some innocent and unknowing victim to talk to and molest. I sink into the crowd and crawl to the bar.

No sooner have I escaped this devil, than I am accosted by another large grinning mug. Faces loom out in front of me as I blink through that dim lighting. It's obvious from the stink of beer and tobacco that I am in the company of complete and utter scoundrels! I turn to leave but my exit is barred by the lolling tongue of my pursuer from the street. His dogs look up at me and whisper to each other in that infuriating doggy language of theirs which nobody but the devil can understand. Apparently it is something personal about me, and evidently highly amusing, as the lady dog (which is the polite form for bitch) laughs, shakes her shaggy ears and looks down her grotesque snout at me in disbelief. The elder dog then whispers some even juicier titbit in her cocked ear, wags his sandy brush-like tail and bursts out laughing. Which only goes to show that no matter what their pedigree, dogs are still capable of the foulest baseness. They must notice that I am watching them for they suddenly grow quiet and look away, the elder dog pushing his narrow muzzle between the lady dog's legs and sniffing away to his heart's content.

Seeing an empty table, I quickly sit myself down and pull my hat down over my eyes.

'You're in my seat, Blue!' A voice growls at me. I look up. It seems that no matter which way you turn in this life, your path will always be blocked by some madman or other ... And he sticks his smashed up face into mine: a great red potato with a snow-white Stetson stuck on top. I immediately jump back up, apologising.

'Excuse me,' I utter insolently, and try to push past this new tormentor, who, instead of just letting me be, decides to spread out his fat doughy fingers as if to catch me.

'What sort of hat is that you're wearing, Blue?' he speaks. 'I sure do like that hat!'

I smirk at him, a harmless fool and again try to push past ... And he grins back at me, baring his teeth, his eyes like little knots of dirt, his hand raised, blocking my way. I see that I will have to humour this mad man.

'And may I say you've got quite a big one yourself!' I grin at him, and his great hands come up and his fingers play with the brim of his great, white hat. The effect is as if a plate of sausages has somehow come to life and started to roll around on some vast deckchair that this fat-faced fool has got jammed on his head.

'That's some hat you've got on there, Blue!' He leans back on his heels, stood there in his lumberjack shirt, his beer-gut sticking out half a mile. About eighteen stone and six foot two of him. And his ridiculous hat stuck on top, brim upon brim of it, about twenty gallons worth, billowing out on top like a vast erect blanket, spreading out over his brows, his silly face peeping coquettishly out from beneath and his jeans sagging at his knees, his little legs jammed into his cowboy boots like two sponge fingers dipped in chocolate.

'I sure do like that hat, Blue!'

It's obvious that I am in the presence of a monomaniac, suffering from some heinous trick of nature whereby all he can talk of is hats.

'How do you do?' I say. 'My name is Claudius, Gus Claudius.' I raise my hat, delicate and pallid by comparison and again try to pass.

He ignores me and shakes his head admiringly, his eyes like tiny, hungry little currants, intent on eating my hat whole.

'Shoot! That sure is a damn fine hat you got there, Blue! Do you mind if I try it on, Blue?' Without hesitating, he steals my little titfer off my head, then reaches back over and plonks his oily great Stetson down over my eyes. It comes way down past my ears. The lights go out and the stink of his decomposing head fills my nostrils.

I have to lift the brim and peek out at the world, like as if I was a Christmas squirrel, who, waking on Christmas Eve and feeling the rumble of hunger in his red furry belly, stirs from his nest in a snow-covered copse of Douglas firs and, rubbing his tired eyes with the backs of his soft paws, looks out wondrously into the strange, snow-covered world, before scampering down the frozen boughs in search of his hidden store of nuts.

My friend stands there with my hat balanced on top of his great scuffed head. He grins and does a little jig.

'Flea! Look at me – look at me! I'm dancing – I'm dancing!'

The girl with the pregnant belly lifts her forehead from the wet bar, flexes her eyes at him, her mouth hangs open, a broken cigarette dangling unlit. 'Give the man his hat back, Blue,' she says tiredly. 'Give it him back!'

He stops mid-jig, looks resentfully over at Flea, then sorrowfully swaps hats with me.

'That's a beautiful hat you got there, Blue, you be sure you look after it. Not many people could get away with wearing a hat like that. That hat . . . it's got character!'

'Leave the man alone! Just shut the fuck up and leave the man alone . . . and get me a drink!'

'Aw, Flea!' He turns to her, a look of hurt spreading across his massive face. I allow myself to be swallowed by the crowd.

Large jets of purple smoke bloom up all around me as everybody smiles their skull-like faces and puffs on their bitter pipes and cigarettes. I wedge myself into a corner and try to make myself invisible.

Just by my face is a small and brave ant walking along the top of the bar, carrying a great boulder of sugar in his vice-like mandibles. He makes all sorts of heroic efforts, at one point coming to an impasse which forces him to double all the way back and take an entirely new and perilous route along the very edge of the pumps. He sniffs at a huge lake of dark mild and one brute almost crushes the poor fellow with his thuggish elbow. I grow more and more agitated by these close encounters with death and have to resist the temptation to push the people away from the bar and knock the sugar lump from the ant's jaws and press its helpless body to the bar beneath my triumphant thumb. A presence looms behind me and Blue drops his smiling hand down onto my shoulder. He shouts to the barman.

'Oi! Blue! Get Blue here a drink!'

Apparently, everybody in his world apart from Flea is called Blue.

The barman looks mournfully up from the far end of the bar. Blue clicks his fingers at him.

'Oi, tosspot, get Blue here a drink!'

I look around nervously. Flea is still sat across the way. She smiles her thin lips at me. Her hair plastered across her forehead like melting plastic, a half-pint of gin in her tattooed hand, the other holding a cigarette across her belly ... Nine months pregnant. I try to smile back at her, but my bottom lip sticks out and I have to pretend to be looking at something interesting in the wallpaper.

The barman waddles up from the far end, puffs out his cheeks, mops at his brow with a wringing-wet tea towel and starts polishing up the bar in front of him. I order a small glass of dark beer.

'The people call me Fat Malcolm,' he whispers to me.

I have to look into his face. His eyes hold me very seriously. That's what it is – everybody's pain is holy!

Fat Malcolm sweats over his bar, great dark patches spread out from under his armpits, a pair of real tits and a belly like the prow of a ship, jammed in behind that little bar. All in all, he gives the impression of a pot-bellied barge that has become lodged in a ridiculously small and inadequate lock.

Somehow, the ant has disappeared, or been annihilated.

Fat Malcolm reverses back and down the bar, puffing and panting. He completes a three-point turn and then sets off again at full steam up towards the barrels at the far end. All the while swearing gently to himself under his breath and mopping at the beads of sweat that race down his sullen cheeks. Blue leans over me, blocking out my light.

'You don't want to drink that dark shit!'

'Blue!' Flea calls to him.

Blue ignores her. 'If you can't drink, don't drink! If you can drink, then shut the fuck up and drink!'

Fat Malcolm backs off the barrels and rolls back up to our end of the bar. He looks at me imploringly, then sadly, his head to one side, places my glass down in front of me.

'So, you think you're a rebel do you, Blue?'

'Blue!' Flea screams and Blue turns.

'Flea, I'm just talking, that's all. I'm just talking to little Blue here!' He turns to me. 'Ain't I only making conversation? Ain't I, Blue? . . . Blue'll tell me to shut up if he wants me to, won't you, Blue? Blue can speak for himself, can't you, Blue?'

He chucks his voice over his shoulder, his eyes returning to me, to make sure that I'm in full agreement.

'You think you've got the rebel in you, don't you, Blue? But you don't even know what the rebel is! My rebel is big! Way big! My rebel, for instance, is bigger than your rebel! I see what you're thinking, Blue. You're thinking that I'm bullshitting you, int'cha, Blue? You think that you, with your swanky fucking hat, know it all, don't you, Blue? But you don't know fuck-all compared to old Blue! You better believe it, my rebel is big, way big!'

'Look into my eyes, Blue. You can't nail me down, can you? I'm here, I'm there, I'm gone! I'm the Blue Clown . . . the Clown has tears; the tears of a clown! He's sad but he's funny!

They laugh, but what are they laughing at, Blue? Are they laughing at him or with him ... Now that's the big question, isn't it, Blue? That's the big question!'

Flea stands. 'Jesus Christ! ... Leave it now, Blue! It's finished!'

'Shut your mouth, you slut!' Blue doesn't even bother turning. He lowers his voice to a harsh, hateful whisper and leans his face into mine.

'That's all they're good for, Blue, the bitches! Put them on their backs, Blue. If they can't fuck then they can fuck off! You see, Blue, I'm an artist. I make my carvings, I make my puppets. I'm the Puppet Master!'

He studies me with his little maggoty eyes and I try to meet him and show no fear.

'So, I make you laugh, Blue. You think I'm a joker, but I'm no joker, Blue. I'm the Blue Clown ... You see, Blue, there's a difference. Are you laughing with him or at him, Blue? That's what's worrying me, Blue. Are you for him or against him? That's the question I've got to know the answer to, Blue ... But be careful, 'cause you never know when the Blue Clown will strike. My rebel is big, way bigger than yours!'

'I've a book in my head, Blue, a novel, a thousand pages, ten thousand pages, who knows? It's not written down, Blue, it's all up here! It's not for sale, you see, no one can buy it, Blue. It can't be written down ... what's it worth, ten pence? Are you taking the piss? ... Or a thousand pounds, maybe? ... It's worth more than you or anybody else could ever afford, Blue. I keep it locked away in here!' He screws two fingers into his temple, raises his ginger brows and stares his eyes at me ....

Flea scrapes her stool back and stands steadying herself at the bar. 'Shut the fuck up! ... If you don't shut the fuck up, I'm fucking leaving!'

Blue clenches his small yellow teeth. 'Well, fuck off then!'

Flea raises her glass, empties it in one gulp, places it back onto the bar with the care of a drunk, belches and wipes her mouth with the cuff of her leather coat.

'I'm going up the fucking hospital to have your fucking baby and you're fucking coming with me you fucking cunt!' she spits.

Blue pulls himself up to his full height, tucks his gut inside his blue jeans and leans his face right into mine.

'So, why do you wear that hat, Blue? Are you bald? Or is it just to try and make yourself look like the Clown? Or is it because you think that you've got a big rebel?'

Fat Malcolm stops polishing the empties and presses himself against the back wall of the bar, clutching at his sodden tea towel. I lift my glass to my mouth and smell its rank odour.

'I told you, don't drink that stuff, Blue!' he shouts, and snatches the glass from my lips.

'Alcohol never passes my lips, true or false?' He juts his fingers at Fat Malcolm.

'That's right,' stammers Fat Malcolm, 'Blue only ever drinks lemonade!'

He turns on Flea, 'What do I drink, Flea?'

'Right, that's it! I'm fucking going!' Flea staggers across the bar and up the little flight of steps, cold air rushes into the room and she disappears from view out of the building.

'And good riddance to bad shit!' Blue turns on me again.

'I've got pictures of the war at home, Blue . . . Cine-film! Super Eight! Videos! You name it, Blue, I've got it! I filmed them! All myself. Film of the concentration camps, Blue. Babies on bayonets, Blue. The whole fucking lot! Sights that will turn your stomach, Blue.' His blood-red tongue darts out, laps at the white scum that collects in the corners of his mouth and his hands come up and his podgy fingers start fondling with my lapels.

'You don't believe me? I'll swear on my mother's grave! I filmed them all myself, Blue . . . that's what the Nazis are doing and it's not fucking funny!'

He stares off into space somewhere above my head, caught in reverie. Suddenly he looks down to see what he's holding in his hands and lets go of my jacket, fear flickering in his hard little eyes.

'Look, Blue,' he says absently, 'when I take my arts troupe abroad, you will come too, won't you, Blue? You're an artist, aren't you? You think you've got a big rebel? Well, Blue? Are you with me or against me? I'll be taking the Blue Clown. And Uncle Ginger Nuts – he'll be in full make-up, the lot! Can I count on you, Blue? When I get my bus, Blue, that's it, I'm off! I'm the Rebel. My rebel is way big! No one can touch it, Blue, 'cos I will die to preserve it! And that's the artist speaking . . . Thirty pounds will buy you a ticket, Blue. The bus costs six hundred. Can I count you in, Blue?'

He examines my face, peering into my soul, daring me to contradict him. The pub grows hushed. I study the flock wall paper, a framed print of fox-hunting . . . Maroon spirals . . . The man with the bullet head stands and shuffles towards the doorway, his rat-like dogs look to me and smirk with their doggy eyes. I am afraid, but not of this madman punching me and knocking me broken and bloodied to the ground, but of him unwittingly exposing some part of me that is so raw and unknown that it breaks in his clumsy great fists and rises up like a black destroying angel to engulf both of us.

Slowly he raises his great sausagey hands and clenches his fists together, his mouth twisting into a delicate sneer. I close my eyes and try to breathe, my intestines swarming like poisonous snakes. Suddenly there is a loud crash, the front door flies back and Flea comes lolloping back down the stairs screaming at the top of her mouth. She throws a punch, winds one up and lets it go – smack! – into the side of Blue's head. Blue ducks and cowers behind me. Flea pushes me out the way and catches him another one, kicking and punching as he goes down. Her shoe catches him a glancing blow in the ear and he drops sideways onto the deck, nursing his reddening eye. Flea stands towering over him, her hands on her hips and her belly out to here!

'Do you want me to drop this fucking baby on the fucking street? Or are you taking me up the fucking hospital, or fucking what?!'

She yells at his head and kicks at him again. Blue scrabbles across the floor, his doughy fingers feeling for his beautiful white Stetson. She looks down on him with contempt, lifts her foot and stamps on his hands.

'My hat!' sobs Blue, reaching out as Flea kicks it across the room. It dances like a white ghost, quite scaring one old lady, before disappearing mysteriously under a far table.

Tears stream down Blue's hot cheeks until we have to look away ashamed, clenching our ears. Flea pulls him to his feet and drags him blubbing up the little flight of steps, out through the banging doors and into the cold night.

HERE STARTS THE NOTEBOOK INSCRIBED
BOOK THE 2ND

I pull my cardboard suitcase from under the bed and open it up on the mattress. Tonight I will copy up my story from my author's notebook and my poem will begin. From beneath my shirts I extract a brand-new unopened packet of embossed business paper, which I borrowed from my father's briefcase on my last visit to my parent's house in the summer.

It is a three-mile walk to my parents' house and I refuse to squander precious pennies on silly bus rides. It's a hot and sticky day and my mother speaks to me in her harsh, hot whisper, which is a signal that my father is at home. Apparently it's the first time that she's laid eyes on the old coot in the last two months.

'Why are you whispering?' I ask her irritably, knowing full well that it is because she is a coward and that she is insane. She looks at me meaningfully and slams the oven door. Then the old man shouts something from the top of the landing and she goes trotting out of the room, obediently clasping onto her old dish rag. There is a dirty plate on the draining board with some bacon rinds and three uneaten mushrooms swimming in a film of grease.

My father doesn't talk to me, he communicates his wishes solely through my mother. I sit around in the kitchen drinking tea, waiting for him to go out into the back garden and start playing with his pathetic lawnmower.

My mother comes back downstairs and holds me with one of her pained expressions.

'What?' I ask her mechanically.

'Have you been climbing in that tree again?' she whispers.

'What tree?'

'You know your father says that you're not to climb in that tree!'

'What tree?'

'I'll give you "what tree?" The cherry tree, that's what tree!'

I watch a fly that comes down off the lamp and lands on the bread board. First of all it licks at a piece of blue cheese, then hops nonchalantly onto the butter dish and marches clean across that vast yellow field to the other side, whereat it dips its vile nose into a great hill of bread crumbs. Finally, satisfied that it has trampled its stinking feet through every imaginable food stuff, it lazily itches its bottle-green abdomen with one of its disgusting hairy legs, then buzzes off to eat some dog shit.

'You broke off a branch!' hisses my mother, 'you're not to go climbing on the roof! There's only roofing-felt up there, you'll put a . . .'

The old man comes downstairs and she trails off. He crosses the kitchen and goes out the back door. My mother lifts her eyes and stares after him. I empty my cup in one gulp, casually saunter out of the room and close the door on my mother. In the hallway I smooth my hands on my thighs then leap up the stairs, taking them four at a time, my heart pounding with ecstasy. I run into his room, snatch up his briefcase, then stand motionless, listening for the sound of his wretched lawnmower over the banging of the blood in my temples. It takes me about thirty seconds to work the combination on the locks: 181, the number of our house, and 195, the number of the house we lived in when I was a kid. I open it up, my chest bursting in sexual fear. Right on top I find an envelope containing over two thousand pounds in brand-new five-pound bank notes. I slip three of those little fellows out of the envelope and fold them away into my pocket.

There are several pornographic magazines from which I select two. I'm just closing the case when I notice the packet of embossed business paper. I remove it, tuck it down the front of my trousers, shut the lid and scramble the combinations.

When I get back downstairs, the lawnmower is still whining away outside and I can see my father's torso through the glass, marching up and down with his head boiling in the sun. I step back in behind the blinds and go to the toilet to examine my new magazines.

The fifteen quid I ingeniously stitched into the lining of my jacket. The business paper, I have been saving for just such an important occasion as this.

I sit down on the floor on my moth-eaten old blanket, light a candle and huddle over its non-existent warmth. I try various positions to keep the chill out of my bones, but find that sitting cross-legged with my jacket over my shoulder is by far the best.

I slit open the packet with my penknife, then, taking the first sheet of paper from the pile, I begin to laboriously copy up and re-write my story, chewing on my tongue and itching some flea bites that have appeared in the night.

Quite frankly my story makes little sense, whichever way up you look at it. Whole sentences jostle for position on the page, colliding mid-paragraph, tumbling over each other and then spreading out into an inky mass to merge into the margins and then even further out, crammed across the bottom of the page. Unpronounceable words appear in thickets, which are then joined by sparse hedgerows of fiercely hatched letters that resemble no written language and ramble on for page after page, in no particular order whatsoever, until finally they die out or get incorporated into a whole new forest of meaningless sentences. I hold the pages in my hands with disbelief.

Whatever has become of my beautiful poem? I spend at least two hours rearranging my notes and knocking the introduction into some semblance of order.

By the time I develop my main theme and come to some sort of a conclusion, I've chewed my tongue red-raw and my jaw is set, locked in such fierce defiance that it aches. Around me sit the stumps of six candles and the ice-blue light of day is already in the room.

My eyes are scalding from it, and my legs cramped into twisted useless appendages with no life left in them whatsoever. I re-read the final paragraph several times, hoping that it might just begin to make some kind of sense to some poor soul somewhere. Then, holding my shaking hand steady as I can, I sign my manuscript and fashion quite a respectable full stop. I sit back and a flea hops from inside my shirt and rattles across the page in front of me. Instinctively, I press my finger down on him, trapping him to the page. Then, slowly exposing just enough of his black shell-like body so that he can't hop off, I crush him with my thumb nail. With satisfaction I see my blood smear across the page. That's me down there! Let it be known that I have signed this testament in blood! Let it also be known that this is how I will treat all blood-suckers!

I try to stand but fall twisted to the bed, my calves and knees locked in cramps. I straighten my legs, screaming in pain, cursing and rubbing my calves vigorously until at last the cramps subside and I can stand on my numb and tingling feet. On reflection, it might have been wiser for me to have sat in my brother's blue nylon sleeping bag. But comfort is not what makes great literature.

I seal my manuscript in an envelope, scrawl the name and address of a publisher across it, then place it carefully into my inside breast pocket. My hat is green. I step into my shoes and head out onto the morning street.

The cars stand bumper to bumper clear up to the end of the high street, their exhausts puffing up into the icy air in great hoary breaths. Setting out into this bright wonderful day, I smile at these poor senseless beasts heading for the self-imposed misery of their jobs. I seriously chuckle to myself, and lightness comes into my step as I waltz up the frosty pavement, overtaking a vehicle every half-dozen steps. Nothing can shake the feelings of goodwill that spill from every pore of my body. Even the stench of diesel and petrol doesn't irritate me and, smiling, I shout 'good morning' to every person I meet.

I make animal noises just to amuse myself and grin in through the windows at the drivers in the stranded traffic. If I could have whistled a tune, I probably would have.

On several occasions I have to stop and check that the envelope is still in my inside breast pocket and smile contentedly to myself. The more I think about it the more convinced I am that I have written a masterpiece. A little gem from the hand of a promising young writer. I hold my head high.

'You live off of social security? On hand-outs from the state?'

'Haven't you heard of me, a young writer trying to make a name for myself?'

'You steal from the hand of your own father, filching from his brief case, behind his back!'

'I took only what I needed, your Honour, only that which is mine by birthright.'

'And you intend to carry on claiming State Benefit whilst also collecting a State Grant from the Academy?'

'Only to tide me over, your Lordship, just until I get the advance for my latest manuscript.' I pat my pocket.

'What about paying your rent then, you little whipper-snapper!'

I question and cross-question myself in this silly manner right the way up until I cross the road at the bottom of Star Hill. It seems that I am intent on spoiling my good mood and forcing myself to admit to the lowness of my nature, no matter what. But the more I goad myself the happier I become, until in the end I am quite sure that I have the blessings of all the artists and saints, right down through the ages.

I do a little jig outside the Post Office and feel the powerful bond of blood that flows through me and links me, as if in a chain, to the great authors of the impossible past. For these moments of truth I feel truly privileged and chosen.

When I look up, I am crestfallen to see that the Post Office is shut. The sign on the door says that the opening time is nine o'clock. I peer at the grotesque 24-hour clock that hangs menacingly in their window, just above the first class posting box. It reads only eight thirty-two, which is an impossible age!

I walk over and check the stamp machine but it's out of order. I jam my finger in the slot but there isn't even a penny lurking around in there. Disgusted, I sit down on the bench and proceed to wait.

Actually, I can't resist a chuckle to myself at the sight of all those shopkeepers arriving for work, unbolting their shutters and setting up shop for the day. How ridiculous they are, puffed up with their own self-importance, totally unaware of the young writer in their midst.

One of my sleazier aspects is laughing up my sleeve at complete strangers.

Actually, I can't help sniggering at my dear friends also. That's something – a vice really – that I enjoy a lot and just can't put down. It's like sucking on a sugary sweet, or getting your fist jammed into a honey pot. People really are unspeakably comic in my opinion, if only they knew how stupid they looked.

Just because in some silly way I think that I'm so much smarter than everybody else, it doesn't necessarily follow that I'm any more arrogant than some other rascal who believes himself to be a complete and utter fool. In fact, because of my inquisitive nature, I'm far more likely to come to some sort of complete understanding of the idiocy of arrogance than any of these other bozos who go around masquerading as so-called intellectuals. Of course, my elders and betters, my school teachers (Mister Shawd, the school proctor in particular), did their uppermost, so help them God, to beat this out of me. But somehow, due to my obstinate nature, I suspect, it remains gleeful and unrepentant inside me, but will still, so my family and friends assure me, have to be smashed out of me.

Presently a little old lady comes along, dragging an empty shopping trolley behind her like a coach of doom. She has a small crutch in her left hand and twists her hips like a sick spider. Evidently one of her legs is shorter than the other and she has what appears to be a hump on her back.

I notice that everybody on the street ignores her without exception. People who were previously completely unoccupied turn their faces away and become suddenly engrossed in polishing their pathetic brass door fittings. But the little old lady seems oblivious to their quiet hostility and all the while smiles to the left and right, twisting along the flagstones towards me. As she draws abreast, I suddenly have the urge to jump up, lift my hat and shout good morning at her. I find myself on my feet and have the strangest sensation that I am looking down at her from a great height, as if I haven't just stood up but have somehow leapt to the rooftops of the building opposite and am now viewing her as if she is a minuscule bug.

'Good morning to you, madam!'

She twists her neck round over her hump and squints up at me, her eyes sparking like flints in her tiny head.

'Why, thank you sir! It is very kind of you to speak to me, kind sir!'

I have to force myself not to wince. I am staring into the mischievous face of a shrivelled old goblin. I smile my eyes at her and clamp my jaws. I have no intention of showing her that I am at all taken aback by her deformed and child-like body, and nod respectfully.

Apparently her lips and eyebrows have been crudely drawn onto her skull by a child's hand, whilst her doll-like hair, that sticks up in nicotine-coloured tufts, has the appearance of having been inserted into, rather than growing from, her scalp. She holds me with her sharp little eyes and keeps her head cocked insolently to one side, obviously soliciting a reply.

I cough and speak equally formally. 'Not at all madam, the pleasure is entirely mine.' And I lift my hat again.

'Oh, thank you, kind sir! Thank you!' She lowers her head, scrapes her shoe across the pavement and bows her tiny body. I cringe in disgust. Her obvious delight at having been politely addressed angers me. Why should she be so pleased to be addressed in such a rude manner by such a complete fake as me! I am a charlatan, whereas she, as a cripple, sits next to God.

I stare up and down the High Street in search of some distraction, hoping that she will soon tire of this inane and pointless conversation. But she obstinately remains bowed before me, as if only I have got the power to break this spell that I have unwittingly cast upon her.

I stare anxiously at the passing faces, seeking some escape or excuse for leaving her, but can find nothing. In desperation I motion to the bench and offer her my seat.

'Oh, thank you, kind sir! You are so kind, sir!'

I stand, waiting for her to sit, but she remains rooted to her spot. All the while smiling up at me like a grotesque child. I am already wishing that I had never greeted this cantankerous old witch.

She clasps onto her small crutch so tightly that the tendons on her neck stand out like cables and her whole hand shakes with violent tremors. The rubber tip of the crutch is as new, and hovers a whole six inches above the pavement.

I had noticed on her approach that she didn't use the crutch to support her in her twisted walk, but rather carried it merely as an ornament, as a security blanket, or perhaps as just another added hindrance – just to make sure that things weren't too easy for herself in her crippled attempt to drag her wretched corpse up and down the high street.

She squints at me questioningly, as if seeking permission to speak. Hating her, that she should presume me her superior, I nod.

'Is it windy, sir?' She speaks. I look at her, barely able to conceal my loathing.

'Is it windy, sir? I don't like the wind, sir, it frightens me, sir!'

I lick my finger, stick it into the air and shake my head. 'No madam, there is no wind today.'

A look of gratitude fills her pale grey eyes.

'Oh, thank you, kind sir, thank you!' And she takes a little step towards me, lets go her empty shopping trolley, and grasps the hem of my jacket with her clawed fist.

I grin nervously and pat her ice-cold claw, searching for some charity and goodwill in my retreating heart, but instead, all I feel is a terrible and fierce anger rising up inside of me. All I can think of is ditching this tiresome old witch before it engulfs me totally.

I look to my naked wrist as if I have a watch and back to her eyes, then ashamed, I look away again.

'If you'll excuse me, madam, I'm afraid I must go,' I lie. Finally, she relinquishes her vice-like grip.

'Oh, pardon me for keeping you, kind sir! Of course you must go now, sir! God bless you, kind sir! God bless you, kind sir!' She paws at my jacket, and for one terrible moment I think that she is going to lift it to her slash-like mouth and kiss it.

Hurriedly I try to stuff my hands into my pockets but they have somehow grown too big. Smiling inanely I mutter that I am late for dinner, bow and withdraw. I step wildly into the street, darting between the fits of crawling traffic. I turn and tip my hat a final time and she remains stood there staring after me, her orange painted lips still mouthing 'kind sirs'.

I push on up to the end of the High Street, cross to the Esplanade and stand staring over the edge into the muddy swirl of the river, and childish thoughts of suicide come racing into my mind.

'Look at all those currents and raisins.' And my father is

holding me up over the river, his blond beard tickling my face as he repeats his stupid riddle, which I never understood: 'Look at all those currents and raisins'.

I turn and cross back over onto the High Street, intent on finding something to eat. I pass the baker's and stand a long while gawking in at the display on the counter before the old bat inside bangs on the window at me and shoos me away, as if I am an unwanted goose.

I thrust my freezing mitts into my pockets and march on, my mouth salivating so furiously that I have to swallow and spit. I follow a girl dressed in high socks, who comes out of the entrance to The Bull Hotel, and is apparently pretending to ignore me. My heart drains out to her just as if I am a bottle of blood-red ink that, with an unknowing swish of her taut, high buttocks, she has knocked from her writing bureau onto some old worn woollen garment with her name embroidered childishly upon the breast. I have to catch up with her and stumble into several gentlemen with white moustaches. I stare at her and make her turn and look at me. My teeth ache for her, and I go down on my knees, my soul ripped out of me by the sight of her magical buttocks. 'Kursty!' I gasp. Then the crowd swallows her and spits out that old witch, who comes twisting her way back along the pavement towards me again.

I jump into a doorway and peep out. She is still nodding and smiling to herself and still dragging that ridiculous, empty shopping trolley behind her like a cart from hell, and her crutch is still hovering uselessly above the gutter. And I hate her all the more for her indomitability and for forcing me to deny her and align myself with all those who I most detest – the very people who had ignored her and rebuffed her in the first place.

I narrow my shoulders and, looking only at the pavement and passing feet, pull my hat down over my eyes and quicken my pace past her, feeling positive that she is indeed the most spiteful and persistent old bag I have ever encountered.

When I next look up I have evidently re-crossed Star Hill, for I am standing outside The Andy Snacks.

I take off my hat and push inside. I go straight to the counter and order egg and chips. The lady who takes my order has a large drip hanging from the end of her nose and I have to use all of my self-control not to reprimand her on the spot. Something, of course, which I would never do. Instead, I smile weakly and ask her for my eating irons.

She picks my coppers from the counter and, counting them out into the palm of her hand, sniffs and hands me a cloakroom ticket.

'We'll call your number when it's ready, love.'

She flings my knife and fork down on the counter so they clang and bounce in front of me, probably more out of slovenliness than any show of contempt. But I still decide to take offence and think peevishly that she has decided not to like me, maybe on account of the cut of my jib, or perhaps just because I have neglected to comb my hair, which apparently stands up on end like a lot of porcupine quills.

She points me towards an empty table. I snatch up my eating irons and stride over, pull out the plastic seat and sit, resting my elbows on the yellow formica table top. There is a paper napkin. I pick it up, sniff at it and stuff it inside my open shirt front. I play chess with the salt and pepper pots.

A man with startling white eyebrows comes clinking his cup and saucer at me, sits himself down with a groan and empties his tea into his saucer. I watch as he bunches his lips together like a dog's arse and sucks on it loudly, licking his lips. He looks at me with his insolent eyebrows and winks. I quickly look down and study my ticket – number 146.

'What you got there?' he speaks at me. I pretend to be so deep in thought that I haven't heard him. I scrunch up my brows and stroke my chin as if on the verge of solving some impossible mathematical equation.

'I bet you're having egg and chips, ain'tcha?'

I realise that, yet again, it has happened to me, that I must after all carry an invisible sign round my neck welcoming all the ugly, disadvantaged, shambling and the lost to come barging in and harass me with their impudent and pointless questions.

I twist in my seat and look over my shoulder, purposely ignoring him.

'I knew it! Egg and chips!'

Exasperated by his inquisitiveness I turn on him roughly. 'Evidently you were standing behind me and heard the lady take my order!'

'That's right, I did.'

I was counting on him contradicting me and am forced into silence by his joyful admission.

'Got any work?' he asks.

'No,' I reply, then feeling the still unposted envelope in my inside pocket, I add mysteriously 'yes and no'.

'That's interesting,' he says pleasantly.

'Interesting and not so interesting, depending . . .' and I look at him mischievously, egging him on into heaven only knows what nonsense.

'I suspect you're a student?' he enquires.

'Not at all,' I lie. Just then the lady calls out my number. I lift my ticket and wave it above my head and she creeps painfully over in her worn carpet slippers, the drip on her nose extending down into somebody's rice pudding.

She finally arrives, drops my plate down in front of me and lets out a tired sigh. The old crust wriggles his eyebrows at me, as if they are a pair of snow-white badgers romping over his forehead in search of their dinner.

Ignoring this tiresome oaf I start right off scoffing the food into my face.

'You'll get indigestion,' he volunteers hopefully.

I grunt, stuffing the chips into the egg and into my mouth with my bare hands. Quickly, I clear the plate and sit back. All that remains is my white of egg, lying there like a piece of vile jelly floating in a sea of grease.

'Are you not going to eat that?' He nods towards my egg white.

I shake my head.

'Can I have it, then?'

I push the plate across the table towards him and watch disgusted as he picks up my unused knife and fork and proceeds to cut the egg white up into neat strips. Then, folding them into elegant little parcels he transports them to his waiting gob, where he nips at them with his blood-coloured gums. The finickety nature of this old crust's manners makes my teeth itch.

'So,' he says, showing me a mouthful of egg white, 'what are you studying?'

'I am not a student,' I repeat.

'What?'

I lean over the table towards him and shout in his ear.

'I'm writing a paper on the legend of the Medway Bog Man!'

He stops mid-peck and raises his eyebrows, which gives the impression of a wise old monkey.

'The Medway Bog Man?' he says, nodding slowly, and then carries on eating.

I look at him, sat there, pecking at my white of egg, like a half-starved gannet. The nerve, that this old egg thief should utter the name of the Medway Bog Man so casually.

'Yes, the Medway Bog Man!' I shout at him again. The people on the next table turn to look at me, but quite frankly, I am oblivious.

'It's a very unique case,' I carry on emphatically, 'and one that science has largely ignored.'

'I thought these mummified bog people were quite a common phenomenon.'

'I can assure you, sir, that there is nothing in the least bit common about the Medway Bog Man ... But I suppose you know the whole story back to front!' I spit at him sarcastically.

'I remember some of it from school and some of what folks have told me since,' he replies mildly.

I unplug my ears and stare at him totally gob-smacked. He carries on chewing his final and most disgusting mouthful, swallows, and arranges the knife and fork neatly on the plate in front of him. He loosens his collar, coughs, sticks his greasy finger into his vile gob, withdraws it, studies his filthy nail and dries it carefully on the leg of his blue overalls.

I peer for any trace of humour on his wrinkly old mug but there is none. He really does believe that he has heard of the Medway Bog Man, and that he even studied the subject at school.

'You must have gone to a very advanced and forward thinking academy.'

'No, not at all,' he replies. 'Actually, I left school when I was thirteen.'

'But it seems that you've studied local history in quite some depth?' I add bitterly.

He waves his hand dismissively, completely ignoring my caustic tone.

'No, no, I just like to keep abreast of local issues. It doesn't do to keep your head buried in the sand does it? Now, this bog man,' he carries on, 'weren't his legs lost whilst they were excavating him?'

I look him up and down. 'No,' I shout, 'you must be thinking of an altogether different bog man. Probably his Russian cousin or something.'

'I'm sure I remember reading that the excavator took off his legs . . . just below the knees . . . Before they quite realised what they'd found.'

'Absolutely not! The Medway Bog Man is an altogether different kettle of fish! He was found at Upchurch, perfectly preserved, clasping a twentieth-century schoolgirl's shoe in his leathery grasp!'

'Is that so?' he says thoughtfully.

'What's more, the pathologist had to break his fingers to retrieve it,' I add ghoulishly.

The man strokes his chin, takes out his tobacco pouch, rolls a cigarette, lights it and sits there puffing out the blue smoke, totally unruffled.

I stare at him gloweringly, studying him for some glimmer of doubt. He taps the ash off his cigarette and clears his throat.

'He was quite some age this bog man, wasn't he? Two thousand years, was it . . . ?'

I narrow my eyes.

'They actually estimated his age to be some seven thousand years old' – I stare at him – 'preserved in a freak fermentation at the bottom of a silted-in creek, or 'palaeo channel', to use the full archaeological term.'

He nods knowingly and coughs again, slightly. I see that I will have to come up with something truly spectacular to ruffle this old coot's feathers.

'Despite it being highly unusual,' I continue, 'to find a peat layer with a pH level suitable for preserving the living flesh of a bog man in an intertidal marshland, by a fluke of nature, or perhaps by the devil's own design, every single pore of his body was perfectly preserved! It was evident from the stubble on his chin that he hadn't shaved for several days. There was even a tattoo of what appeared to be a crude Mesolithic gallows still clearly visible on his upper arm, and the remains of his last meal, a form of Stone Age muesli, still lay partially undigested in his lower gut. His neck had been snapped and he was pushed into the creek and evidently left to drown.'

The old crust merely nods and seems to be quite at home with my description.

'You do understand the ramifications of this discovery?' I hiss at him. 'We're not just talking about any run of the mill old corpse here, we're talking about the living flesh of a Mesolithic man, equipped with hunting bow and two mud-encrusted hell hounds!'

'Oh, the dog . . .' he muses.

I can't believe my ears and hate him all the more, for his naivety and gullibility; that he just sits there and hasn't questioned one single jot of my story. I can no longer tolerate this vile old crust believing every word of what I say and decide to force him, by hook or by crook, into denouncing me as a liar.

'The Bog Man, or Thee Medway Bog Man to give him his full title, was unearthed in 1936 whilst the police were searching Upnor Marshes for the missing schoolgirl Kursty Morgan. Her body was eventually found some fifteen years later, after the death of one James Lovecroft, gamekeeper and armchair archaeologist – who was coincidentally a tireless campaigner to keep Thee Medway Bog Man in north Kent. Kursty's perfectly preserved body was discovered, still fully clothed, in a sealed cot in Lovecroft's attic. The only item of clothing that was missing was her left shoe.' I look at him pointedly. 'The mystery was further compounded by the nature of Lovecroft's demise, namely that his death had been brought about by the forced ingestion of the toadstool Amanita Virosa, more commonly known as The Destroying Angel. No one was ever convicted of Lovecroft's murder, though rumour has it that his housekeeper and cook, Patricia Coltsworth, was none other than Kursty Morgan's great aunt.'

My wise old monkey strokes his nose.

'That's right,' he agrees, 'I remember it now. Fungus poisoning.' And he puffs out another bitter mouthful.

I feel a tickling sensation somewhere in between the back of my throat and the depths of my right ear and bang myself on the side of the head with my fist. The nonchalance and unshakeability of this old crust completely outrages me and I decide to drown him in dates and fabrications, to see just how deeply this vile rascal can be drawn in. I place my elbows on the table top and lean my face into his.

'I suppose you think that I've made this whole story up from start to finish, don't you? I suppose you think that there never was a Medway Bog Man and that I've just been sitting here stringing you a line for my own entertainment? . . . This is not just hogwash or hearsay!' I yell at him. 'There were reports in all the leading journals of the time, he was running around naked with his neck snapped and his head on backwards, for God sake! Go and read them for yourself if you don't believe me!'

He sits back with a look of bewilderment in his eyes.

'No, I believe you,' he implores me. 'I can even remember going to see the body with my father before the last war. I was just a boy, I must of only been about – what – eight or nine. He was on display at the old museum at East Gate House, before they moved it to the Guild Hall. Then the war came and I don't know what became of him . . . I believe he was put into storage in case of invasion or incendiary damage, I suppose.'

I stare at him, completely floored by this fantastic new revelation. Incendiary damage, my foot! This spiteful old crust is intent on stealing my creation away from me – from right under my own nose, so to speak.

'I think I might still even have a postcard of him indoors. I

could look it out for you if you like. Do you come in here often?'

I realise that I will have to muster up all of my powers of invention to snatch my Bog Man back from the thieving grasp of this unscrupulous individual.

'You seem to know an awful lot about this Bog Man,' I humour him, 'so I presume that you are familiar with the incident when he escaped?'

'He escaped?' The old crust pinches his furry brows together, looks sulkily out at me and scratches at a gravy spot on the table top in front of him.

'Yes,' I rush on excitedly, 'on the night of the 14th of April, 1942, on the seventh anniversary of his discovery, during an air raid. When the guard returned from the corporation shelter, he discovered that the Bog Man's glass case had been smashed open and his muddy foot prints, and those of his two hunting dogs, led out onto the main stairway, down the hallway and out through the front door.'

'Surely you mean he was stolen,' reasons the old crust.

'No!' I shout triumphantly, banging my fist down onto the table. 'If you remember, the police report stated quite clearly that the cabinet had been smashed from the inside; the glass splinters covered the whole room. The bolts on the front door were thrown and the latch lifted – from the inside. No traces of a break-in were ever found!'

The wise old monkey leans forward thoughtfully and shakes his head. I fold my arms, puff out my chest and stare intently at him, daring him to contradict me. He looks down at my empty plate.

'It's true,' he mutters to himself at last, then turns to the next table. 'I remember it all now, the whole mysterious incident.' An old lady and her little white dog nod to him consolingly.

'But the story didn't end there,' I cry maliciously, 'not by a long chalk, it didn't.'

I decide to teach this old rascal a lesson he won't forget in a hurry, to smash him from the field of play once and for all, for having the nerve, the audacity, to try and steal my Bog Man! I rub my hands together and my victim smiles up at me timidly.

'Shortly after the Bog Man's escape,' I elaborate, 'various incidences came to light to suggest that the Bog Man hadn't returned to haunt the marshes, as the authorities had originally hoped, but that he was in fact living in the vast labyrinth of tunnels that criss-cross beneath these very streets, and that he was intent on causing as much mischief within the city walls as was ghoulishly possible!'

'Now that, I know, is fact!' pipes up the dry old crust. He speaks to the whole room, still greedily intent on stealing the mummified ghoul of the marshes. 'All the forts are linked by tunnels, from here to the dockyard; some say there's even one that runs clean under the river!'

I glare at him, forcing him to shut up, then carry on with my magical story.

'His first hideout is now known to have been in the caves under Amhurst redoubt. At night he would re-enter the city via Fort Pitt and the Delce Tower. Fantastic rumours started spreading of a mud-covered ghoul seen accosting schoolgirls on their way to and from school. There was even one report of a twelve-year-old child having her school shoe fondled in broad daylight!' I pause and tear at my thumb nail. 'In an entirely separate and unrelated incident, the original guard from the East Gate Museum swore he saw the mud-bedecked ghoul in broad daylight, cunningly disguised as the town crier. The guard duly waylaid the suspect and, after trying to tear off its fake whiskers, was beaten, kicked and chased by the ghoul, roaring and spitting fire up the whole length of the high street. Fearing for his life the guard ran into the Two Brewers public house, where he insisted that the landlord double bolt all the doors whilst he recouped himself in the bar. Wherein, he remained ensconced until morning. Several Officers of the Law were in attendance and vouched for the sobriety of the witness. And he later attested, on oath, that it was indeed the very same Medway Bog Man, and not a look-a-like impostor, as some skeptics had suggested.'

The old man shrinks smaller and smaller with each new revelation I make. And whereas before, he had had an air of amenable friendliness, now all he can muster up is a bitter smile. I stare at him, daring him to refute me.

'Reports and sightings of the Bog Man continued right up until the early nineteen-fifties,' I gloat. 'Sightings and molestations became so common that even the church became involved and the Cathedral was forced to employ the services of one Reverend Arnold Trescott, pot-holer and professional exorcist, aided and abetted by his three accomplices, the Bunion Triplets. They were given strict instructions by the Bishop, the Mayor and City Council to recapture the Bog Man, dead or alive, and return him forthwith to his display cabinet, along with the museum's missing collection of Iron Age pottery and artifacts.'

By now the whole cafe has grown hushed and turns to listen to my wonderful tale. I grow more and more exuberant in my descriptions, until my friend, the thief, with his snowy-white eyebrows, slides from behind his table and makes towards the door.

'This they almost succeeded in doing on the fifth of November, Guy Fawkes night, 1956!' I scream after him. 'Listen to me!' I yell at him, shaking my fist. 'Listen to me, you damned thief!' And the poor wretch stands there dithering in the doorway, neither coming nor going, explaining himself to anybody who will listen.

One of the serving ladies comes over and tells me to sit down and quieten myself. She touches my arm very lightly and it is as if a bolt of electricity shoots through me. I collapse to my chair, hold my head in my hands and rock back and forth, sobbing uncontrollably for the loss of my youth, for the theft of my marvellous creation.

That my nerves were completely shot through was obvious. It now became clear to me that eating too much protein was what was at fault: the yellow of egg was evidently too rich for my liver.

The serving lady leads me from my table and takes me out back. My whole frame is wracked with cold chills and I sit there trembling for what seems like an age.

She tells me not to be a silly boy and that her name is Dot. She brings me a large mug of hot, sweet tea, but rather than helping me dry up, her kindness sets me off on another weeping fit and I cry so pitifully that she holds my head in her lap and my tears wet her apron.

'The Reverend Trescott was lucky to escape with only a severe mauling,' I blather, 'and the Bunion Triplets are still in the madhouse, to this very day!'

'Yes dear . . . I know dear, it's shocking, shocking . . .'

She strokes my head and I erupt into another torrent of self-loathing, berating myself and apologising for crying . . . that I don't know what's come over me. My eyes are blinded . . .

great strings of snot cascading from my nose. I stand and she takes my hand and shows me to the toilets, where I sit shivering for half an hour blowing my nose like a bugle.

Sooner or later, we all have to step back out onto the street – that strange place of meetings and loss – where everything will eventually have to happen.

My throat was raw from shouting but otherwise my good mood of the morning was still alive within me and I decide to put this minor setback behind me, go forth and post my manuscript at once. I stride off in the direction of the Post Office, wiping my tears on my coat sleeve. My mind is so chock-full of contradictory thoughts and impulses, which are plainly too absurd to follow, that I have to concentrate my mind by chewing on my tongue, which is simply a habit that I have had since childhood and have no reason, as far as I can see, to let go of. Although I'm sure it hands my many enemies another convenient stick with which to beat me.

I am aware of a little white dog looking sardonically up at me, which makes a whirring start up in my brain and quite involuntarily my right arm rises up into the air in a ridiculous salute and the dog says to me, 'You will keep your right arm up in the air for the rest of your life!'

I look at the dog in disbelief and laugh for pulling such a cheap stunt on myself. Obviously, this must be some preposterous idea that I have picked up from reading some vulgar magazine or other.

I try to lower my arm and put my hand back in my pocket, where it will be out of harm's way, but I can see quite clearly that my hand is intent on staying exactly where it is, hovering in space, and resolutely ignoring even my simplest instructions.

It should be noted at this juncture in our story that the world is full of strange and improbable happenings that we often find amusing or baffling, or even completely beyond the pale. But that does not mean that they are in any way false or are to be held up to ridicule, or treated as mere dreams or fantasies. May

I just warn you that I begin to feel a malignant dread creeping right across the back of my neck and downwards towards my heart. My legs tremble and my knees knock together like conkers. I walk on, my arm swinging above me like a mast, doing my best to ignore the clamour of voices that scream inside of me. But the more I nail the lid down on their insulting chatter, the louder they yell. I arrive back in front of the Post Office and have to bite my knuckles just to stop myself from screaming. Of course, it is Saturday and I see that the great double doors are closed tight shut, the office having closed at half-noon for the rest of the day.

Swearing at the top of my voice, I kick at the postbox and fall onto the bench, my arm still flung up in the air. I stare at it in disbelief. I feel sure now that some vile and malevolent forces have been unleashed against me for no other reason than I am my father's son.

'Yes, why shouldn't you walk around with your arm stuck up in the air all day? For the rest of your life, even!'

No, fate has not been kind to me for quite a number of months now but for the last two weeks, in particular, I have been set about by a whole gang of disasters and peculiar calamities. Actually, I am not in the least surprised that my arm should be controlled by the telepathic wishes of some unknown white dog. Indeed, it would not surprise me in the least if my poor arm should just dry up and wither off completely!

Sitting there on that bench, humiliated and beaten, I imagine that I understand the nature of my curse: that somehow I have sinned against the very nature of my genius by revealing the contents of my wonderful story to those wretched imbeciles back there in the cafe.

I kick myself, worrying away like an old woman itching at a scab that is never allowed the time to heal. The more I think of it, the more convinced I am that some sorcery has been unleashed against me. It all makes perfect sense, the old man with his ridiculous snowy-white eyebrows and that cantankerous old hunch-back asking me this and that about the wind! They are in cahoots and together they have put a hex upon me.

Didn't they both have the same mischievous glint in their vile, smudgy eyes? In fact, they could, for all I know, be one and the same person. One agent of evil in two different, and very cunning disguises. But not different enough to outwit me! Hadn't the old crow only pretended to need her silly crutch? And didn't the little talking dog share the same hair colour as that scoundrel in the cafe? I make impossible leaps of the imagination, finding all kinds of sinister coincidences to link the three of them in their vile conspiracy. Anything to keep the dark thoughts at bay that kept jostling in my befuddled brain: that truly it was me who had sinned, by uttering the name of my own creation in such a public place, merely to humiliate a decrepit, lonely, old man, and prove that I was smarter than him.

I try to pull my right arm down with my left hand, just so's I can blow on my poor mitt, but it absolutely refuses to budge and just stays there, jutting out into the distance like a plank.

'Now you're just playing silly games with yourself,' I admonish myself, and I can feel myself growing convinced that I could, in fact, lower my hand if I really wished but that somehow, without knowing, I have promised myself that I never will.

'Which is just a lot of tommy rot!' I shout at a small boy who just happens to be passing with his mother. In his hand he carries a gaily coloured windmill on a stick. He quits blowing on it and stands and stares at me, then his mother snatches up his hand and leads him away, looking over her shoulder at me.

I really try to smile at her but I needn't have bothered. Already, along with the rest of the sickening bunch, she had me marked as a leper. I sneer at her. I don't know who she thinks she is kidding. By just one glance at her preposterous backside it is clear that she is as ignorant as the day is long.

'So now you have finally managed to make a spectacle of yourself!' I shout after her and gaining no response, stamp on my own foot in punishment.

To compound everything, the fingers of my saluting hand begin to itch and throb, (the blood had supposedly drained from my wrist and an aching numbness spreads across my back and shoulders).

I turn and face the back of the bench and sit there like a twisted scarecrow willing my hand to drop back into its natural position. But no matter how I reason with myself, apparently its obstinacy knows no bounds.

Next up, a pigeon with a club foot decides to stomp its deformed leg all over the pavement in front of me. It really does do everything in its power to distract me and flies directly at my face. Then, landing in the gutter, it walks painfully towards me, pecking like a clockwork toy at bits of nothing on the pavement. The wind ruffles the feathers on the back of its neck and I raise my foot and make as if to kick it. It flinches and takes off sideways, then flutters back down onto the kerb and starts weaving its way back across the flag-stones towards me again. It is taunting me, hobbling on its horrible, gnarled claw, mimicking me and laughing from its silly twisted beak. I gob on the ground and it flutters, lifts its bedraggled head, gallops over and starts pecking stupidly at my feet.

'Can't you see that I could quite easily stamp on your ugly head and break your stupid beak?'

A Post Office truck goes past and an old grey-beard comes and sits down beside me. He does a little circuit of the post boxes, four bright medals glinting on his chest, then, farting with concentration, parks himself down on the bench beside me and scares my pigeon away. I wave my poor arm in his direction but he doesn't even seem to notice and instead stares resolutely ahead, intent on ignoring my affliction. I stand slowly, turn and stare at him, giving him ample opportunity to say good morning and apologise for his rudeness, which he refuses to do. Muttering, I turn and storm off, cursing the day this ignorant old warmonger was born.

I cross back over at the bottom of Star Hill and head back along the stream of traffic, thoroughly defeated, my arm waving about like a flagpole. Some schoolchildren in the street start laughing at me and a lady in a yellow coat even goes so far as to pull her lap dog away from me when I try to pet it, which is unjust.

Just before I get to St Bartholomew's Terrace, a car slows down and a youth with whisky-coloured hair throws a rotten egg at me and his friend screams an obscenity as they speed off.

'So now you are known to all and sundry as a complete and utter fool! Will you now take your arm down?'

A group of workmen look curiously up into the empty sky to see what it could be that I am pointing at and then shout 'Heil Hitler!' at me before telling me to clear off.

By the time I finally arrive at my front door, I'm limping around like a sick lamb. I fish out my key on the end of the string round my neck, put it in the lock and duck inside.

It was the exact right door with the exact right door number on it, everything.

Neither asleep nor awake, I lie twisting on my bed in a sea of sweat, my arm stretched out above my head, propped painfully against the headboard. I run through that same dark landscape, dragging my guitar case behind me with its dead cargo and the knowledge of my certain incarceration weighing heavily on my heart, and then a man clothed in mud bites my neck.

I open my eyes, starting in panic. The skin of my neck is snared in the zip of my sleeping bag. I lie here, my heart pounding, swallowing on my spit, terrified of some unknown revelation that stands poised like an assassin behind a gossamer veil, threatening to smash into my consciousness with every passing second.

Fearfully, I unzip my brother's sleeping bag, kick it from my legs and roll from the bed fully clothed, my mouth dry and sour, my nose full of snot. I hobble across the darkened room and drink from the tap. A flash of electricity shoots through my right shoulder and into the numb mitten of my hand. I groan in exasperation.

'Why in God's name should I be chosen to suffer such an affliction? What terrible crime against nature have I unwittingly committed? So I was born bad! So it's in my karma, but isn't anybody going to explain to me the rules? Or do you just go around picking on any poor soul and start tripping them up just for fun. Handing out a hunchback here and killing a small child there? No, no matter which way I look at it, I can think of no earthly reason why I should be singled out for punishment, so in God's name, why pick on me?'

I open my door and slip downstairs like a thief. I can hear the sound of hard irregular breathing coming from the basement below. I lift the latch, let myself out onto the street and silently pull the door to behind me.

The night is completely bound in a thick, clinging fog that seems to permeate everything it touches, giving the effect that the whole street is weighed down and waterlogged. I hear footsteps running in the distance and then a loud crash comes from behind the cemetery wall. I have to force myself not to re-open my front door and sneak back upstairs to my stinking mattress.

I swoon on the doorstep and rest my feverish brow against the damp and sodden brickwork. I lick at it and eat a little shred of moss.

'Let me sleep here,' I say to myself, 'and drink my fill from these bricks like blotting paper.'

Actually, I look to my ridiculous arm and great confusion rages through my tired and oversensitive brain. The events of the day twist themselves into an intricate lattice-work and superimpose themselves on top of one another until I'm not quite sure what I really am or who it is that is thinking.

I pull myself to my feet and have to keep repeating over and over to myself that I have been chosen for a mission, though I don't for the life of me know by who, or for what. Keeping close into the buildings, I set off up the alley towards Fort Pitt, my hand still waving in the air in its salute. I have to gasp in pain, my heart dragging like a stone.

I dart across New Road and pick my way up past the college, following along the wall of the old blockhouse. Noises of night birds, that quite obviously should be asleep, keep barking at me from out of the bushes and seem intent on mocking me from the safety of their tree tops.

Suddenly, in front of me, the wall is swallowed up into a vast toothless mug and I take a nip on my quarter bottle before entering into the tunnel. What little light that had been held by the fog immediately falls away and the darkness swallows everything. Everything comes from darkness and everything must return to it. I breathe it in and swim in it like ink.

I walk into the tunnel's mouth, speaking to myself continuously, forcing myself to picture the vilest of crimes and murders, as if they are taking place right here in front of me.

It seems that I am absolutely determined to drive myself out of my mind and picture whole racks of decapitated heads lining the walls beside me and laugh as I accidentally kick over a bucket of children's hands in the dark. The more terrified I become the more I gloat, my fevered mind forcing itself to dream up ever more vivid scenes of torture and all manner of night beasts hungry for my blood.

'There is nothing to be afraid of,' I say, trying to comfort myself, but then I refute myself and deny it. 'You are for the high jump now, you idiot; that worm you trod on is about to grow into a dragon!'

I carry on this constant battle with my own wits, harassing myself at every turn, determined that I suffer for some terrible backlog of wrongs that stretch back over the centuries and which, for all I know, I never even committed.

My feet shuffle over broken bottles and fallen masonry, and I refuse to allow myself to light a single match or to even think of turning back.

'You're going to get your brains smashed in,' I say laughingly, without so much as a hint of compassion. And so I taunt myself at every turn.

'A spider is eating your shirt!' I say out loud, and a chill runs down to my very bowels. I have to check and brush at my shirt, trying to flick any fat dusty spider to the floor without breaking open its blood-heavy body.

'Where's your muddy friend now? Has he stood you up?' I can see that I am teasing myself unnecessarily with this provocative questioning and point blank refuse to answer. I feel my willy through my trouser pocket and squeeze it, then command myself to shout out loud at the top of my voice: 'Are you there?' The sound of my voice terrifies me in its closeness, echoing around the whole chamber, filling my ears like a hot liquid.

The wet nose of a hell hound brushes up against the back of my hand. I snatch it away and a pair of eyes that burn like fire hover before me.

'Good dog!' I whisper.

I turn my face and decide that it isn't really dark in this tunnel at all and that in reality the tunnel is well lit, but out of the perverseness of my nature I have chosen to keep my eyes tight shut, just to spite myself.

I feel my face, and then force myself to stick my thumb in my eye. I feel my eyeball and wince. My eyes are definitely open, but then I change the rules and convince myself that I haven't really made sure properly and that they are, after all, closed, and that I am a sissy and a coward, and that I will have to feel them all over again to be absolutely, totally, certain.

I carry on like this for two or three minutes, forcing myself to touch my eyes again and again with my cold and dusty fingers, until they are burning red and my cheeks are hot with tears. Finally, satisfied that I haven't been lying to myself, I allow myself to walk on, the fingers of my left hand walking along the crumbling brickwork beside me.

'Are you there?' This time my voice sounds strangely removed and I have the peculiar sensation that I am listening to my voice from some far off distant place.

I hold my breath and listen. I am not alone. Another creature is close by. I hear it slithering across the floor in front of me, writhing on its slippery belly. A noise rattles in its throat like a spider scuttling in a crisp packet and a nauseating odour of black river mud rises up to me and something warm and clinging rolls in my stomach.

I vomit into my own mouth, clamp my jaws and swallow, my nose and eyes stinging. Then it rises within me again and a great stream of bile jumps out of me. I stand jack-knifed against the wall, tears wetting my face, my stomach knotted, as hot jets of liquid spurt from my stinging lips. I clench my fists and madly gasp for breath, but again my guts twist another great retch out of me, and I feel certain that I will never breathe again and prepare to die here in this urine-soaked tunnel.

I panic and fall to my knees in the juice. I cry out into the night, swearing and chewing on my lips. I bite my tongue and howl in pain and a terrible and undeniable anger soars up from my bowels and out through the top of my skull. That I, William Loveday, should be treated by God in such a way. And I stand and charge headlong into the blackness, my legs carrying me along at a terrifying pace. I can feel that shadow man pursuing hard behind me, his breath spurting at my neck. I run on and on, my legs flailing out like rubber bands, all the while babbling to myself, accusing myself of the vilest cowardice, until I force myself to stop, turn and allow my pursuer to catch me. I feel myself slow down, then turn and wait for his stampeding feet. To feel him smash into my very essence. To feel his arms entwining around me as he powers into my chest, every black pore of him oozing river mud and decay.

He holds me cheek to cheek, his lips biting at my neck and throat and I gag and lunge, kicking him away. I scrabble to my knees, moaning and cowering from his merciless onslaught. This vile creature has been haranguing me at every step, tormenting me and making all lightness black. I squat down, huddle into a tight ball, then launch myself where I suppose his stomach to be. I push off with my feet and collide headlong with the wall opposite, a great light bursting inside my skull.

Dimly, I become aware of the taste of sour blood in my mouth, my head pounding, my lips coated in dry brick dust.

I pull myself up onto my scuffed knees and start to paw my way along on all fours, my limbs frozen. Bits of fallen masonry cut into my hands and knees until I have to stand and shuffle along supporting myself with the wall.

I stop and feel the fingers of my right hand, and suddenly my heart swims with joy and tears spring to my eyes. The curse on my author's hand has been lifted! And a little voice in me rejoices. I sit there in the dark, running my fingers over my palm and gripping my wrist.

'It seems that you have won your hand back from that filthy ghoul, you have done battle and won the right to your hand!'

A black splinter in my consciousness has shifted, a delicate crack of sunlight broken through, making my heart tremble in gleeful anticipation, and a raging fire of sunlight opens up before me and I stand to my full height and run hobbling towards the tunnel entrance. The town lies spread at my feet before me, the river curling like a worm in the palm of my hand.

The river is always waiting for you in this town with its arms outstretched and its grim smile, bits of broken wood, stumps and rotting jetties. A plume of black smoke rises up from the distant dockyard and is shredded on the wind.

I walk out onto that field – a crow jacks its body at me and cries three times in recognition – my eyes squinting in that cold harsh light, and I laugh and dance a little jig, raking my fingers through my caked hair and banging the clay from my knees. I shake out my jacket, then suddenly, my heart sickening, I feel for my manuscript. I run my fingers through all of my pockets. I look in impossible creases but it is definitely gone. I pick through all of my pockets once more, desperately beating my jacket till clouds of dust rise into that golden dawn, then throw it down in disgust and pace back and forth cursing myself. I turn and run back up the pathway lined with brambles, towards the tunnel. I peer blindly into that cavernous mouth, but my quest is hopeless, I have no idea where I ran in that night of twisting labyrinths. And anyway, I already know the identity of the thief, the reek of his body is still on me, that stench of sour mud as he cuddled me in his slippery arms, every black pore of his body oozing foulness. It would have taken him only a second to slip his wretched hand into my jacket pocket and relieve me of my manuscript. I shake my head in disbelief. Who could have reckoned on such guile and cunning from a corpse? His tongue, like a black slug, clicking against his empty gum . . .

'I am Oliver,' he spoke.

There is no letter from Kursty in this morning's post and the postman crushes a harmless snail beneath his thuggish boot, I suspect on purpose. But I did get a small official-looking envelope with the stamp of the Academy emblazoned ostentatiously across its entire front. My name is misspelled and written in a curious childish scrawl. Immediately, curiosity burns up inside of me to know the contents of this mysterious letter.

My face seems hideously ugly to me and I find fault with all of my features and even go so far as to punch myself quite hard on the nose. I have to repeat this several times until at last I feel pain. I mess my hair up, pull at my ears and make rude faces at myself. On the whole I think my face to be ugly in an interesting sort of way, which is not a contradiction.

My brother's cheeks are like a pair of cream puffs.

During my absence the junkies in the basement have broken into my room, rifled through all of my possessions and stolen two long-playing records from my childhood. I also detected that the rest of my meagre belongings have been picked through and sniffed at, but luckily they have left my brother's red leatherette guitar. Presumably on account of it being worthless. No matter what my brother says of this incident I shall never return it to him.

Some friends of mine at the Academy have a music group, but singing and performing, in my opinion, is just a cheap way of showing off. I am learning to play the guitar, though my parents and a whole string of failed educators assure me that I lack all musical ability and talent and am, in fact, tone deaf. I have also been practising my singing. My dream is to be adored by a loving and admiring audience, though I would of course also loath this.

The letter from the Academy says that I have chosen to withdraw from the art school, which is silly, as I have never chosen to do anything. It goes on to state that 'A course that is structured to cope with 84 students must take into consideration the interests and objectives of the majority and it is in protecting these interests that we have found it necessary to call into question your attitude of total rejection'.

I screw the letter up, toss it into my empty provisions box and walk round the room, pulling at my imaginary moustache. On my next turn, I pass the box, extract the letter and smooth it out against my thigh. There is no doubt that it is official. Oh yes, it's the real thing, signed, stamped and dated! '... by banning you from these portals and refusing you access to the photocopy machines, we are also saving you from certain prosecution under the Obscene Publications Act!'

I peer suspiciously at the Principal's signature. It is possible by this alone to see that the letter has been penned by a pompous and ignorant barbarian. I fold the letter and place it carefully in my inside jacket pocket. The papers will come to hear of this outrage against one of our emerging geniuses!

My grandfather is eighty-five and has just been admitted into hospital. He ran away to sea when he was thirteen and was a sailor all of his life. He was blown into the sea at Zeebrugge during the First World War, was at the battle of Jutland and the only man in the Baltic who didn't grow a beard against the

cold. He said that I can have his medals when he dies. He has a tattoo, shiny shoes and hands like big, dried-out spiders.

When my father was a little boy his hair was so blonde that it was in fact white, and the kids on the street used to call him 'Snowball'. And when my grandfather used to come home on leave from the Royal Navy, he would hit my father and his sisters with a leather belt, then lock them down the cellar. Probably my grandfather will die. He lives in a small terraced house in Gillingham with an outside toilet.

I had my tattoo done today; it is all in black and of a hangman's gallows. Tony, the tattooist, made a comment about its ghoulish nature which secretly thrilled me. It didn't hurt me in the slightest, though there was blood and I had to grit my teeth. The noose is not quite drawn properly but Tony tells me that this is on account of it being blown by the wind.

My father used to stuff a handful of blue five-pound notes into my grandfather's spiderish hands when we used to have to go and visit them at Christmas, which is undignified. My grandmother had a half-pint mug of gin and sherry and my father said that it could knock out a horse, but she said that on the contrary it tasted very nice and that it was a shame that he only came to visit them once a year.

I asked my grandmother if I should take my grandfather anything special up the hospital when I go to see him and she said to take him a can of beer. At first I was going to take him a can of lager but then decided that brown ale would probably be more to his liking.

The fact that my grandfather will soon be a ghost worries me a little bit, but on the whole it doesn't. Everybody has to die but nobody knows what being dead means. This room, for example, is haunted. Some nights there's such a din that comes in off the street from disembodied spirits trying to smash their way into the pubs at closing time, that a young man can find it difficult to sleep. I am excitable and sensitive by nature and will not stand to be ridiculed. Children's graves are by far the most scary.

Today I will stop the world:
After I have been sitting here for over twenty minutes the bus finally decides to show up. I climb on board, pay for my ticket and drop to a seat. The lady opposite has a large blackberry-coloured birth mark spreading out across her neck and down over her chin.

I smile grinningly at her and she drops her gaze, her eyes flinching and bruised looking. Instantly I feel anger rising up the back of my neck and have to stop myself from shouting at her. I was only smiling, for Christ sakes. I didn't mean anything unkind. If she could only smile back at me, then maybe the worst evil in the world would be forced to somehow become good.

I feel my tin of beer cold in my pocket. We jerk to a halt and about ten more people clamber on board with their idiotic bags of shopping. Last of all, this lady with bleached hair and a broken mouth comes dragging her pram up the gangway. Two snot-nosed kids hang onto her coat, jamming ice creams into their faces. I grin at this sea of grey faces that traipse past me. An old man sat opposite looks to the lady with the pram, tucks his unshaven chin inside his overcoat like an old stoat and closes his hooded eyes. I, on the other hand, immediately jump up and offer the lady my seat. I sweep off my hat with a flourish, which in the circumstances seems very noble of me, and I smile to myself and slap myself on the back and tell myself that as long as William Loveday rides the buses of Chatham town the age of chivalry is far from dead. Although I make light of it, I thoroughly understand that this is, of course, the correct thing for a gentleman to do.

I turn and roll up to the back of the bus, grinning fiendishly at my travelling companions, who sit stroking their vast hooters like a bunch of holy Buddhas.

And then I see her – my princess! She is beautifully sat alone, her scarlet hair tied back in a plait, like a great hissing snake. And upon her feet a pair of shiny red shoes. I have to stop myself from falling to the floor and grappling with her delicate white ankles.

I sit down next to her and wait for her to kiss my cheek. I imagine taking that plait in my hand and kissing it like it was some great heavy cock. A wonderful feeling of naughtiness spreads across my chest, down my arms and out through my tingling finger tips. I drop my bus ticket on purpose and watch it flutter down onto the deck between her feet, then snatch it back up and wave it under her delicate nose.

'Excuse me, miss, did you drop your ticket?'

She looks at me, her eyes hot with recollections. I turn quickly to a little old lady with a dog and shout at her.

'I believe, madam, that you have misplaced your ticket?'

The little old lady gives me a ferocious grimace, baring her teeth like so many needles, and her little dog snarls up at me, its eyes rolling in its head like a pair of black marbles.

Everything within that gaily coloured carriage conspired to intoxicate me. It must have been the effect of all the chrome and aluminium fittings. My excitement grows more and more intense, until I feel that my chest is about to explode of it. I accidentally kick the back of the old lady's seat and both her and her mangy mutt fix me with withering stares, then, as one, they turn their fist-sized heads and point their eyes like poison darts out through the dirty, rain-streaked window. We swing around a corner and head up a steep hill, the winter sun going like a yo-yo at the dirty glass.

'What coarse-minded people they allow on public transport these days!' I blurt out loudly to myself, and indeed it seems that I am on board a bus to Hell, with nothing better than a bunch of scoundrels as my travelling companions.

'Standards have been slipping!' I shout. 'I will be forced to make a report to the Mayor!'

It seems that my mind is highly volatile and it doesn't take much to send it racing off in ten different directions all at once. Again I stroke my can of beer and hold its cool surface to my brow, just to remind myself who I am and to bring myself back into my twitching body before I head off on another loop.

'I know that you all have mind mirrors!' I say out loud, and sit staring ahead of me, trying to marshal my scattered thoughts and come to some understanding of what I have just said. I run this new idea of mine over in my feverish mind, examining each fragment of thought and trying to ascertain just where it can have sprung from. The mind is a delicate mechanism, I tell myself, it needs exacting and specific nourishment or it can fill itself with the strangest ideas and most outlandish of notions.

'What stop is this?' I whisper to Scarlet.

'The Brook,' she answers timidly.

'These people think that I don't know that they all have mind mirrors!'

She looks into my eyes, her delicate mind desperately trying to make sense of my ravings.

'What is your name?' I ask her.

'Kursty,' she whispers.

I sit back and nod. Of course it was Kursty. What other name could it be?

'Kursty,' I say, 'your father, and probably everybody else, thinks that I am mad. But you must understand that I have enemies afoot and they are hell-bent on my destruction. Can you imagine, Kursty, that my friends and enemies are in cahoots? My manuscript ... my poem, which I was going to dedicate to you, my love, has been stolen by the devilish hand of some foul and unknowable creature, which by some trick of nature they have managed to turn against me!'

This new twist in the tale delights me and I gloat as I see the terror register in her dear eyes.

'It was dead, this creature, Kursty. I gave it life and now it returns to haunt me!'

I giggle at myself, appalled at the sickness that crawls within me.

'Don't you see that together my friends and enemies might, by some unknown sorcery, come to know everything about me?' I look at her, tears welling up in my eyes.

'Surely you understand that, Kursty? That it is possible that someone, somewhere, has invented a mind mirror, which of course is ridiculous, but that doesn't mean that it doesn't necessarily exist, does it? Everything, after all, is possible, and even if they haven't yet perfected the technique, it's still perfectly possible that one day perhaps they will ... or even the DHSS, perhaps even your own mother will force me to give myself away unknowingly. By making some innocent gesture I could expose the workings of my wretched soul, and all of my desires will be spilled out into the open for everyone to see. Like the guts of a chicken.'

I sit back and start cackling out loud, surprising myself at my fiendishness. I let my head drop to her shoulder and I bite at her plait.

'Help me, Kursty, help me!'

Clumsily she takes my hand in hers, her lips trembling, a blush spreading across her beautiful cheeks. I lift my head and turn on my fellow passengers, clasp hold of the back of my seat and roguishly let myself dribble down my chin.

'You think that I don't know that you've all got mind mirrors?' I shout, 'you think that I don't know that you can look into my darkest thoughts? You think that I'm mad, that I'm sitting on this bus amongst you strangers and that I don't know that you all have mind mirrors!'

I rise in my seat and address the whole bus.

'Well, speak up, or do you still insist on pretending that you don't know who I am, and thereby allow others to believe that I am a lunatic? To believe that I am a nobody, that I'm nothing! Isn't that just a little savage of you?'

Kursty pulls at my jacket, trying to restrain me, pulling me back down into my seat, but I shrug her off, my mind hot with a new intense certainty.

'Go on, cross your gangrenous legs and hold your newspapers to your noses like I'm invisible, all the while secretly studying me with your hideous, disrespectful, hypocritical mind mirrors! Ignore me then, damn you! But don't think for one minute that I don't know all of your names and addresses, you scallywags!'

The bus slams to a halt and I run up to the front. The doors wheeze open and I jump down onto the pavement, free.

The bus driver shouts at me and I laugh into his angry eyes. Everything is crystal clear to me, I am fully aware of my madness, and, smiling, I take off my hat and bow deeply to him and the bus as it pulls away. And I see Kursty, her face pressed against the dirty window, her eyes full and beautiful. I beckon to her but she shakes her head. I watch as the bus pulls up that terrible grey hill and out of sight. I wave but she is gone.

I turn and walk in through those stone gates. This is the hospital where I was born and where my grandfather lies dying. I sit on the front steps, exhausted.

'You're shagged,' I tell myself. 'You need sugar and salt or you'll get the cramps.' I listen to myself in disbelief.

'But I don't get the cramps,' I say under my breath.

'But they're sure to come,' I reason.

I decide to torment myself for ruining my opportunity with Kursty back there, for forcing myself to expose the blackness that lies in my heart and at the bottom of everybody's sweet soul.

'You had your chance my friend and now you've blown it! Now you will never know her, it's over, finished! And all because of your pig-headedness and stupidity!'

I'm furious with myself and am about to give myself a right good pasting, when I notice a sweet young nurse stood by the car park entrance. In my delirium I fancy that she is cupping her breasts and blowing kisses at me. I smile and wave.

'See what you've done now with your inane ravings? Drawn attention to yourself! She is laughing at you my friend, not blowing kisses!' I point this out to myself most reasonably, and on the whole I am pleased with this more diplomatic tone I have taken with myself.

'Can I help you?'

I look up. It's Nursey.

'No, no, I've just come to visit my granddad.'

'What ward is he on?'

I tell her the ward and she offers to show me the way. I tag along behind her. Her starched white uniform talks to me in whispers. We go up and down corridors, across numerous annexes and then up some iron steps and then she turns to me.

'This is his ward.' She smiles.

I tip my hat with one hand and jam the other in my pocket to give her a tip, I close my fingers round a monkey nut, pull it out and offer it to her.

'Would you like a nut, miss?' I say, and start to cry.

She takes me by my trembling hand and leads me into the staff nurse's office and sits me down. A male nurse called Michael gives me a cup of tea. My nursey asks me my granddad's name and looks him up in their register. She assures me that he's going to be okay. It's not that I asked her to check, but she insisted on it.

'Your gran is visiting him at the moment, do you want to wait till she's gone? Or would you rather go along now whilst she's still here?'

'I'll go now,' I say quietly, back-handing a tear and sucking on my snot.

'What have you been doing to yourself?' Nursey grabs my hand and studies my cigarette burns, 'and your face?'

'It's training for my tattoo,' I say, grinning at her. I roll up my sleeve and show her. 'It's a gallows,' I explain.

'That's a bit morbid, isn't it?' She furrows her pretty brows and my ears burn red and I glow with pleasure.

'I suppose you like that, don't you?' She says teasingly.

I nod at her and show her my fucked teeth, my hand comes up and I sob again. Nursey squeezes me with her eyes.

'You go along and see your granddad now, before visiting time's finished, and no more sad-sads you understand?' She holds me in her tender gaze, her little cap perched on her head, and I feel my chest starting to quake all over again.

I turn, quickly open the door, and dash out into the corridor nearly knocking down an old man who stands there dithering with his walking frame. All sorts of tubes and wires emanate from under his dressing gown and empty into an array of little bags and bottles that swing mysteriously from his walking frame.

He grins two little yellow stubs at me, his head nodding all the while, like a naughty little dog who as a special treat has been allowed to sit up on his mistress's lap during afternoon tea, and is being tantalised beyond endurance by the sight of any number of sugared treats and iced bonbons that his mistress keeps stuffing feverishly into her delicate, scarlet-painted gob, only pausing now and then to brush the excess sugar from her fingertips, and tickle his pink and hairless underbelly.

I come to the end of the row of iron beds and my grandfather lies there in the last one, flat out on his back, his little
blue tootsies crossed. It appears that he has shrunk to the size
of a new-born baby. The Sister comes along and sternly tells
him to uncross his legs, this instant!

My grandmother sits there on the opposite side of his bed
wearing her pale blue raincoat and clasping her shopping bag
on her lap. Her hair sticks up like a pile of smoke-coloured
candy floss. Neither of them seems to notice me, or recognise
me. My grandfather has purple-black stains spreading over the
backs of his hands and I can see the smudge of his tattoo on his
forearm.

'Look, it's Ray,' speaks my grandmother distractedly, then,
dropping her head on her shoulder, she reaches out her hand to
clutch at my granddad's fingers.

'Who?' asks my granddad.

'Ray . . . my brother, he's come to see you, Charlie.'

My grandfather gropes his bedside cabinet for his glasses, puts them on and stares at me.

'That's not Ray,' he says. 'Ray's dead.'

'Dead?' speaks my grandmother mechanically.

'Yes, dead. That's not Ray, that's one of your grandchildren, that's one of Reg's sons.'

'Nick?' she asks.

'William,' I say. 'I brought you this.' I hand my grandfather the can of beer; his hand reaches out for it and then he winces and his arm falls back down onto the bed.

'Put it there on the cabinet for me,' he whispers, 'don't let Sister see it.'

I put it down and run my fingers through my hair and smell them . . . I try to arrange my parting.

'So, how have you been?'

'Fine.' I say.

'How's school?'

'He's left school, he's in the dockyard now, Char'.'

'So, how are you getting on in the dockyard?'

'I left the dockyard, I'm at the Academy now.'

'The Academy? And what do you do there?'

'Painting,' I say, 'why are you in here?'

'Damned if I know. Something to do with my blood they say . . . All I know is that I'm browned off! I can't wait to get out of here and go home.'

My grandmother cocks her head at him. 'They'll let you out when they're good and ready, Char', you just concentrate on getting better.'

I wait for a moment in respectful silence.

'What's your tattoo of, granddad?'

'This?' He pokes at the blue smudge on his flabby forearm, 'a bowl of flowers, I think. I tell you this much, don't ever go getting a tattoo, the worst decision of my life that was.'

'You listen to your grandfather,' my grandmother chips in.

I stare over her head at my nursey who is standing in the

doorway at the end of the ward. She gives me a little wave and I blush.

'How's William?' my grandmother says, fiddling with the basket of soft-looking flesh that hangs beneath her chin.

'Nick,' I say. 'I'm William. Nick's OK.'

'And your father? I was hoping he would come in and visit your grandfather when he's not well.'

'He's busy, Aggy,' growls my grandfather. 'He hasn't the time. He can't be traipsing all the way down here, he's got a business to run!'

'But still, you'd think he'd make the time. What's he doing up there in London all hours?' She points her eyes at me.

'I don't know,' I say tiredly. A man up the end of the ward is trying to take a piss in his bed. 'I haven't seen him.'

'What's wrong with your face?' she questions me.

I bring my hands up to my lips. 'I fell over,' I reply.

'Looks like a funny sort of falling over to me.' She puts her chin to her chest and huffs knowingly.

I look to my granddad lying there like a new-born baby, and her perched at his bedside like an old crow, and a sadness sweeps over me and through my entire being.

'Anyway, I thought I'd come and see how you are, but I've got to go now, I've got a lecture this evening.'

'That's all right, you don't need to hang about on my account. I'll be all right, they say that they'll let me out before the weekend.'

'They'll let you out when you're well, Char',' says my grandmother.

'Anyway, I got to go.' I reach over and shake his hand. My grandmother gets up, walks round the side of the bed and lets me kiss her on her spongy old cheek. She presses a cold fifty pence piece into my hand.

'Towards your bus fare,' she says in a meaningful whisper, winking at me and blocking the view of my grandfather with her shoulder. So's that he can't see the transfer of the magical coin. I smile at her, turn and leave.

'And don't go getting any daft tattoos,' my grandfather calls after me.

Outside, the sun is shining with a peculiar intensity. I look up and down the street studying the shadow effect and decide that the sun is indeed burning with a deathly vividness which I have never before encountered. I look up at the clouds which hang there like black slabs of meat ready to drop from the skies and crush the ugly rows of terraced houses that fart their way up the hill side. Actually, I tell myself, they are beautiful. I feel that the sky is in fact laughing at me, which is nonsense, but it is true to say that the sun is glinting at me with a roguish grin.

There is a piece of skin hanging off the roof of my mouth which makes me want to cough. I try to get a hold of it with my thumb and forefinger and give it a tug, but I can't seem to get a grip, so instead I play with it with my tongue.

I walk down the hill and try to blot this nonsense about the sun from my mind, but it keeps haunting me. For several minutes now it has been hiding behind a cloud shaped like a burnt pork chop, but now it bursts forth from its hiding place and accosts me arrogantly. I glare up at this new and totally unfeasible phenomenon of light.

'It is a well-known fact,' I say to myself, 'that you must never stare into the sun with the naked eye. But, nevertheless, this is exactly what I want you to do. The sun can scorch out the delicate optic nerve within a matter of seconds, but you are to ignore this and stare into its depths without blinking, or you will be punished by God!'

Foolishly I obey myself, and stand there and open my eyes directly into the sun's hot arrows, but then I flinch and quickly look away, temporarily blinded. I instantly punish myself for this cowardice and press my thumbs viciously into my aching eye sockets. Again I lift my face and force open my eyes into the sun's direct light. I make myself repeat this experiment three more times before I am truly satisfied that I have indeed studied the very surface of the sun and allow myself to fall back against the wall, white discs floating before my eyes.

'If you are ever to win a woman you must pay for it! If you are going to wank yourself off like a hot, naughty little dog, then you must pay for it! Now walk on as if nothing has happened.'

My original intention was not to tell you anything of my family, but rather to keep you guessing. One thing's for sure, I will always remain a mystery. If I like to pretend that I know everything, that's my problem. From this day on I will quit trying to prove my intelligence and self-worth, and will instead only endeavour to show the depths of my idiocy.

Some days I feel incredibly grown up and adult, and then I have this irresistible urge to break something precious.

'You're a stinking reactionary!' shouts my brother, which makes me feel very proud.

My childhood happened so long ago now, that I suppose that quite soon people will start trying to tell me that it never really happened at all, which is a very stupid thing to say. What they really mean, I suppose, is that time either flies like the wind or else it congeals around your ankles like mud.

I'm terribly sentimental at heart and would like nothing more than for young women to cry whilst reading my poem. I imagine that they might even start sending me little notes or love letters, which I wouldn't be able to stand. And because of the intense passions that my poem would arouse in their heaving bosoms, their men wouldn't even be able to get angry at me, and would instead have to shake my hand and smile at me through half gritted teeth.

Of course it's silly to dream like this, but it's also harmless and a little dangerous. If, as has been suggested, I know no shame, then I wouldn't blush, but I do, which is also a sign of pride. Pride is the thing that needs to be smashed, or rather, it needs to be held and cherished in a mocking sort of a way.

The disgusting thing about writing, in my opinion, is that it's aggressive and unnecessary and proves nothing but the conceit of the person who writes it. As if by somehow crying in public authors have proved their own personal misery to be so much more persistent and noteworthy than the next man's, woman's or child's. This, coupled with the delight authors take in their own cleverness at transposing their pathetic thoughts down onto paper, is what really casts them as the lowest type of villain. Actually, writers are born liars and thieves, only being outdone in their wickedness by publishers and editors. Which is harsh of me, and I apologise. But one thing is for sure: so-called 'well crafted' prose stinks worse than a ton of dog shit.

What really seems to scare readers the most is the fear that their stupidity will be exposed, that they might have been spun a line or even sold a complete dud. So they put on their spectacles, shake out their loud napkins and start asking a lot of boring and impertinent questions as to whether a book is fact or fiction. As if history isn't fiction, and the most preposterous piece of nonsense that you could ever dream up doesn't drip with sad, undeniable truth.

I am well aware of all the insults that have been levelled at me over the years by self-appointed experts, trying to elevate themselves by poking fun at my expense, and I hereby warn them that they should shut their disgusting mouths once and for all before they get them filled! You would think that it was obvious by just one glance at my noble forehead that I am possessed of great wit and intelligence, and that once seen it would never again have to be re-stated. I can only conclude that you can never underestimate the ignorance of teachers, poets and artists in particular.

Looking over the lines I have just written, I would like to apologise. I hereby take back all that I have said that might be thought of as hurtful or impolite. I am not so big as to be unable to admit that I may have been wrong or harsh in some of my observations. And I would also like to take this opportunity to apologise for any distress which I may have inadvertently caused my good friends and enemies. I have a sharp and merciless tongue, I know, and some would say a vicious and cowardly nature. Others might even go so far as to say I am duplicitous and have no real intention of apologising at all, that I'm merely rubbing my hands together with glee and pouring salt into the open wound whilst laughing mischievously up my sleeve. May I say that this is a most hurtful and foul allegation and one that I refute most vigorously.

Someday, eleven o'clock:
Apparently there has been a blizzard during the night and this morning there's a drift of snow running along the inside of my window-sill, forming a little mound on the mattress by my feet. I kick it off onto the floor and make a snow ball.

Today I will exercise.

I went for a walk out on the street and the whole town is in breathtaking chaos. Cars won't start – catastrophe! The little businessmen run around in near panic, slipping and slithering in the snow in their girl-like shoes, their trousers jammed up the cracks of their arses. I have to suppress the urge to giggle and instead laugh straight in their faces.

'There's no milk!' A mournful cry goes up. Someone sobs and again I have to hide my mouth with my hands.

Further on up the street a pitched battle ensues between two old bats, each of them pulling on opposite ends of a pitiful stale loaf. They growl and bare their crooked teeth at each other. One of them, equipped with particularly sharp elbows, hooks the other a vicious blow to the ribs. Her victim takes a sharp intake of breath, then, regaining her composure, crashes her iron-like handbag down on the other's head, thereby snapping her jaws tight shut and causing the poor old lady to bite clean through her own tongue. She goes down on her knees and drools scarlet into the snow.

'That's my loaf o' bread you scabby old bitch, now give it me!' and she socks the other old witch right in the kisser.

All in all, they start nipping at each other's throats like a pair of half-starved dogs, who on first acquaintance seem to get along quite amiably, but after sniffing at each other's arses in their doggy fashion, they happen to notice an injured and septic rat lying prone in the gutter, whereupon total war ensues. Attaching themselves to either end of the unfortunate rodent they proceed gleefully to rip its living guts out, neither of the fearsome beasts being entirely satisfied until the sorry mouse is completely torn asunder.

'Give me the loaf!' screams the poor old lady, blood dripping from her chin.

'I saw it first, you thieving cow!' rejoins the scabby old bitch. Whereupon her grey and cantankerous husband sets about the poor old lady with his walking stick. Presently, a policeman is called.

The park was full of children and I had to abandon my breathing exercises.

When I arrive back at my address some children have made a snowman across the street. I have to suppress the desire to walk over and mock it. I eye it malevolently, then turn and unlock my door. These days my mind is full with all manner of unnatural and disgusting desires.

I haven't eaten anything for two days. My stomach tells me that I am hungry but I know that it is only my imagination. The imagination can do amazing things, even convincing someone that they are starving, which I am not.

This weekend I am going to go back to my parents' house for Sunday Dinner. There will most probably be Roast Pork with Apple Sauce, Roasted Potatoes, Yorkshire Pudding, Boiled Carrots and Boiled Cabbage.

My mother is a short dark woman. Apparently the dog is dying.

On the telephone I told her, 'The world is only how I feel it to be.' But then again the opposite is equally true.

Eating is a disgusting, vile habit used mainly to bully children. My father hates food and hates children. Children are spiteful, dirty creatures, and grown-ups are out to smash them.

I walk down to the market and stand by the fruit stall. There is a whole reef of scarlet pomegranates piled up to the awning. I step forward, pick one of them up and start examining it microscopically, intent on somehow owning it. But the old crone stares at me, a fag sucking in her great gob, daring me to even think of stealing it. I place her wretched pomegranate back on top of the pile and smile weakly at her. If I ever become rich, I will walk up to her stall and buy every last pomegranate in the entire market and then give them as gifts to the handicapped children of the parish.

Finally, I'm down to my last digestive biscuit. There is nothing else left in the bottom of my provisions box, bar a heap of empty nut shells.

Today I have been busy assembling a collage of the findings I have made under the bed and inside the empty wardrobe. Roguishly I rip off a piece of wallpaper from above my headboard and spit onto the floor. I add a matchstick and a picture of a dial cut out of a pamphlet explaining how to check your electricity meter reading. I then kick the wardrobe door in and pull down the landlady's hideously vile curtains and sit back contemplating my total disrespect for other people's property.

I chew on my tongue viciously, examining all the possibilities, then eat my last digestive biscuit, clasping it in my hands as if it is a nut and I am a squirrel sniffing the air for predators.

Tomorrow I will have to visit my father's house, which I shall never do.

Last night I dreamed again of the dead girl in my blue cardboard guitar case. A terrible dread filled my entire being. Wherever I ran in my dream, I had to lug that blue cardboard case behind me. I trudged through the landscape of my childhood, over field and stile, black with the certainty of my guilt, terrified by the inevitability of my arrest, trial and incarceration.

I awake in a sweat, quickly dress and run out into the streets. 'There are no ghosts!' I tell myself, 'only figments of the imagination.' I now fully realise that the world doesn't really exist, but is only created in our own sorry, miserable, misguided heads.

The bitterness of the night punches me. The ice air drilling the fillings in my head and stabbing at my lungs.

The jeweller's clock clicks: 3 a.m. The darkness flows about me in great waves and dense purple shadows rise upwards into the night sky. My eyes water profusely, the cuts in my cheeks smarting as the salt finds them.

Just opposite me, on the other side of the street, stands a man, shimmering in the glow of the street lamp. He leers at me with his black eyes and crooked nose ... I stand stock-still.

'There are no ghosts,' I repeat to myself, 'only the imaginings of a feverish and diseased mind.'

I clench my fists in my pockets and casually cross the road towards him. I keep my head down and view him from beneath the brim of my hat, draw up in front of him, turn my shoulder as if to pass, then suddenly twist and bite at his nose. I rip it from his face and kick him viciously about the body several times, then breathing heavily, stare into his black unseeing eyes.

'There are no ghosts!' I scream at him, 'only the imaginings of a diseased and feverish mind!' I kick at him again, fuming with rage at this rogue's impudence. 'Don't look at me!' I scream and smash my fist into his stupid face, 'I will not tolerate any of your insolence!' I turn and walk on.

Quickly I turn to make sure that he isn't following me, then run back and knock his stupid block clean off his shoulders. I stand gasping over him. 'How dare you contradict me, you sheep in wolf's clothing!' I hiss through my bared teeth. I bite at my raw knuckles, check up and down the deserted street and spit on him. A light comes on in the window opposite. I clamp my chin to my chest bone, thrust my hands in my pockets and run hell for leather up the side alley, my legs flaying out like windmills.

The streetlights stream past me. I hold my breath until I reach the next lamppost, then clinging to it, heart pounding, I stand gasping, bathing in its saintly light. And so I move on up the street, running from lamppost to lamppost, the darkness chasing after me like a great black bird, until finally I stand beneath the shadow of Fort Pitt, and the last light leaves me. I pull my hat down over my ears and press on up past the gaping mouth of the tunnel and onto the moors beyond.

Presently, a fine powdery snow begins to fall and I turn up my collar and kick at the undergrowth. I take a short cut and end up in the arms of a blackberry bush who is intent on not letting me pass. Then the snow starts to fall hard and thick, and the wind, just to amuse itself, picks up handfuls of snow and flings them into my face, right in under the brim of my hat.

I cut across the allotments, climb the spiked railings and jump down onto Boundary Road.

Hungry little animals gnaw at my insides and wave their tiny antennae in a blatant attempt to harass me and force me to lose my way. They flex their grotesque little abdomens and squirt jets of unpleasant acidic chemicals at my insides – in short, they go to any lengths to distract me from my voyage.

I turn right into Maidstone Road and the full force of the blizzard hits me square in the mug. I hunch my shoulders, stuff my poor chilled hands into my pockets and force my way up the hill, step by step. A car comes spinning past me in slow motion, its headlamps look at me drunkenly then pass out with a muffled thud into a large snow drift. On several occasions my feet slip from under me and I have to cling to small shrubs and bushes and use them as levers, pulling myself along on all fours, the snow piling up against my chest and slithering down under my shirt like cold, icy tongues.

I pull myself to my feet and stand at the top of Waterworks Hill. I lick at the snow and hide some of it in my pocket. There's no traffic sound now, only the crump of my own footsteps, which sound strangely in that silent world. The sole of my left shoe is now almost completely off, and scoops up great mouthfuls of snow in its insolent mouth, which then gleefully entombs each of my toes in little jackets of ice.

At the bottom of the dip, in an impossible tangle of hawthorn, I detect the movement of my black panther. I see his silhouette picked out against the snow, snaking between the boughs of the trees, feline and hungry, and I have to run on through the ice, really as if I'm pursued.

Finally, after strenuous efforts, I draw up outside the front gate of my parents' house and peer in through the trees, straining to see any welcoming lights or signs of life, but there are none. I push against the gate but the snow has piled up behind it and I have to climb over. The sole of my shoe gets stuck on the gatepost and I have to slip out of it and jump barefooted into the little drift on the other side of the fence. I retrieve my shoe, stick it back onto my numb foot and walk in under the snow-bound trees.

There are fresh tyre-tracks in the driveway, a number of footprints, and the twisted wreckage of what appears to be my father's car lies arranged on the front lawn, like some futuristic sculpture. I brush off the thick crust of snow and read the number plate – 1 WKT – that's his Roller all right. The car must have overturned and crashed down on the passenger side, and now here it lies, concertina'd, like a half-eaten packet of biscuits. A flurry of wind rises up and whistles high up in the chimneys and a low mournful howling starts up from the pack of huskies that live next door.

It looks like the engine is in a separate display all of its own, stood up on a little plinth under the apple tree. Oil oozes out of the sump and bleeds into the snow like black blood. The possibility that my father is now a ghost floats into my mind and I stand back from the oozing engine and look fearfully towards the darkened house. An uncontrollable shivering comes over me and I walk round to the front door, but the whole place appears to be boarded up for the winter.

The more I stare at that forlorn hanging lantern swinging in the front porch, the more it seems certain that my father has murdered my mother, then faked his own death in a car crash, and that soon, in the not too distant future, I will have to see the ghost of my mother's naked, strangled body walking towards me, her crotchless knickers stuffed in her bloody mouth.

All the doors are locked and bolted, and the only other way in seems to be through the busted top window of my old bedroom on the first floor. Then, my legs buckling under me, I fall to the ground.

I lie with my face pressed into the ice. My nose is burning. The howl of next door's huskies rises up into a terrifying crescendo. I grunt and jerk myself onto my side, roll over onto my back and stare up into the towering night.

Solitary flakes of snow fall through the darkness and strike my stinging eyes. I blink through their onslaught, but refuse to

allow myself to shut my eyes. Suddenly my heart is gripped by a terrible panic and I see that the world has turned dangerously upside-down. I grip my fingers into the snow and claw through the ice in an attempt to hang on. My throat emits a stifled cry. People are only clinging to the surface of this planet by the tips of their stupid toes. Don't they realise that at any moment they could lose their precarious footing and drop off into the bottomless pit of the universe? I stare into that terrible void, from the depths of which some foul and unknown adversary is hurling white-hot boulders into my smarting eyes. My head spins and I puke. I cough and retch, my sore belly knotting, trying to chuck up, but there's nothing down there, so I spit instead and eat some nourishing snow.

All at once the huskies fall silent. I lift my head and strain my ears. Somewhere, beyond the sound of the wind playing tag in the chimneys, I can hear an ominous and distant swishing sound. The same dreary sound that haunted my childhood. It is growing louder and louder. I twist my neck and look this way and that. It is coming from the alleyway that runs down by the side of the house. I know that sound, it is the sound of The Old Man Ghost. On cold winter's nights that spectre rises from his grave and, cursing under his breath, pulls his fathom-long carcass up and down the alley, dragging his gammy leg behind him. His aggrieved spirit is searching for us kids, to catch us and punish us for throwing snowballs up at his bedroom window on the night that he died.

I hear him hacking, then he spits ... the sound of his withered leg swishing behind him. My heart collapses. No matter how hard I try to push these dark thoughts from my mind, I still gloatingly force my brain down onto the hot-plate and conjure up ever more terrifying demons to prowl the night.

I try to roll over and pull myself to my feet, but just wriggle here on my back, my legs kicking up in the air like a helpless bug. It feels to me as if a bony hand has somehow forced its way into my rib cage, got hold of my trembling heart, and is intent on throttling the life out of it. I gasp for air, sobbing silently to myself.

'Forgive me, Old Man Ghost, we didn't mean to kill you. To mock you, or torment you on your last night on earth. It was my brother, not me. I was only the look-out. I was only doing what my brother told me to do, Sir Ghost!'

I speak to myself under my breath, my lungs aching with fear, and then I have to laugh. I giggle and fill my mouth with snow. Evidently I had called the ghost 'Sir Ghost', just to make my speech sound silly and so invite the wrath of this angry ghoul. I wrestle with my insubordinate mind and promise to check my cheeky nature. Hee, hee, hee.

'You murdered that old man!' I yell.

'No! I didn't, I didn't!' I start jabbering to myself.

'You're losing it now,' I say. 'Soon you will die of exposure and it will serve you right!'

I laugh at this new callousness that I display towards myself so openly, and tears course down my cheeks like rivulets of hot lava.

'I love you, Kursty,' I blubber. 'Don't leave me!' I sob into the whiteness of the ice.

'Help me, Kursty, help me! Come back here for me or I'll kill you, you bitch!' I snatch up a handful of snow and fling it at the bushes. So, God disguises himself as a bush? Then destroy me, you fucking bush! Come on, if you're up there. Kill me, you chicken-liver!'

I lick at the snow that covers her beautiful feet, and make believe that my snow princess is standing here before me. I crawl upon my hands and knees and beg her for forgiveness. But she pushes me aside with such harshness, that I let out a little whimper.

'If you will not forgive me then I will die for you, you heartless slag! This young writer will freeze to death here on this spot because of you, you vile harpy! And then, maybe, just maybe, I will be able to freeze my shrivelled heart, to make it an ice-cold stone, cold enough so that it will match your own.'

I clamber shakily to my knees, stand and charge head first into the cherry tree, smashing myself about in amongst the lower branches. I lick at the trunk then bite a strip of bark off and spit it out onto the snow. Actually, my gums bleed. I stand there staring at the strip of wood spell-bound, as if it's the first piece of cherry bark I have ever eaten.

'You idiot!' I yell, 'now you're eating bark, and cherry bark at that!' I slap myself round the face and leap into the tree. I cling on with my raw fists and swing to and fro like a monkey.

'Get up the tree, you idiot!' I address myself.

I hang there and pray for the silver flying saucer that lazily revolved over the house one summer's afternoon, in the distant past of my childhood, to magically reappear over the trees and for it to embrace me, take me in its arms and rescue me from this hell.

I lose my grip, fall back down into the snow and lie there panting like some poor, wretched dog whose master, labouring

under the erroneous belief that this hound has been fucking his bitches on the lawn and pissing up the leg of his master's mahogany bureau, unjustly banishes the innocent puppy to the wilds for ever and a day.

The sound of the withered leg being dragged through the snow is almost upon me. I close my eyes, waiting to feel the bony fingers of The Old Man Ghost stroking my collar.

'Get up the tree!' I yell again. Whimpering, I pull myself to my feet and stand there shivering, my shoes and clothes wet through. 'Get up the tree!'

I jump up, clasp onto a low hanging branch and a great avalanche of snow shakes down on top of me. It goes down the back of my neck and up the sleeves of my shirt. In short, it finds my naked, vulnerable body.

I feel a pawing grasp on my left ankle, my heart empties and I scream with the sensation, kicking out wildly.

'Fuck off, you bastard! Leave me alone!' I clamber up onto

a higher perch, hanging on by my chin, my feet slipping on the frozen branches.

I reach out and make a grab for the guttering, swinging out in that frozen air. I grip hold of an icicle and slowly heave myself over onto the sloping roof. I lie there with my feet in the gutter, my teeth chattering. I crook my neck and peer down into the shadows at the bottom of the tree. There is a miniature wizened face there, made out of a thousand tiny twigs. It grins laughingly up at me.

I stretch out to my fingertips and edge slowly along the dormer windows towards my old bedroom. Curling my numb fingers round the windowsill, I heave myself up through the snow-covered slates, then, hooking my left leg up over my shoulder, I pull my body up and stand with my face pressed against the frozen window-pane. I gingerly nudge the little top window and it clicks open. Now all I have to do is jam my head through there and drag my freezing torso in behind me.

I pull myself up, swinging in mid-air, my arse and legs kicking out into cold space. I accidentally head-butt an icicle and it breaks off and falls spear-like into the night below. I swim through the darkness, but someone has hold of my belly. My fingers find the high back of a chair and I try to pull myself in, using this as a lever. The window catch tears into my soft underside and I groan and make little thrusting movements with my hips. Finally I unhook myself and edge my belly and thighs in through the tiny window, inch by inch, until only my feet are left outside. I cling on by my toes, then crash down into the edge of a bedside cabinet. I'm blinded by a great white flash and lie there motionless, listening to the aching silence of that house.

I feel the steady pulse of blood, as it oozes from my forehead. Slowly I stand and shuffle blindly into the room, feeling the walls for the light switch. I click it back and forth. Nothing.

'Of course,' I yell at myself, 'why shouldn't the electricity be cut off?'

If a domestic pussycat had been tormented and stood on from kittenhood, it would surely come as no surprise that, after its death and subsequent burial, it pulled its rotting corpse from out the ground and decided to terrorise its tormentor by scuttling around between his legs and moving like a mysterious shadow in the corners of his eyes.

I find the stub of a candle and feel for my matches with my dumb fingertips. There is a cat in this room and an uncontrollable wave of shivering passes over me, my hands rattling like skeletons. In fact, my whole body jumps up and down with spasms, my silly hands pawing uselessly at the entrances to my pockets.

I stick my tongue in my jaw and concentrate, but basically my teeth are chattering away so wildly that I bite on my tongue on several occasions. Eventually, by scrupulous efforts, I manage to stuff my freezing claw into my damp pocket and hook my thumb and little finger round the soggy corners of the matchbox. Then slowly, bit by bit, I start to extract it. Twice, with only a fraction of an inch to go, I lose my grip and the matches fall back again into the depths of my bottomless pockets. On my third attempt I wait until the last possible moment, then snatch my hand up and outwards, sending the box flinging across the room and scattering matches to the four corners. I fall to my knees crying to myself, clenching my jaws so as to stop them from chattering.

I manage to find part of the broken box and retrieve half a dozen matches. Then, holding them like daggers, I drag them across the floorboards and eventually one of them bursts into flames. Gibbering to myself with glee, I light the candle stub.

I sit there huddled on the floorboards, cupping my lifeless hands round that miserable flame until my fingers are black with soot. Gradually my teeth stop chattering and my breathing grows shallower and shallower. I become very tired and my head starts nodding. I let myself lie down, curl up on the floor and snooze there. I feel my cheek against the bare floorboards. The cat has left the room and my body quits shaking with quite such uncontrollable shivers. Presently a pleasant feeling of comfort and release spreads through my icy limbs.

I am walking through my father's house carrying my blue cardboard guitar case: I have killed a little girl and her tiny, bird-like body lies hidden inside. I mount the stairs, cross the landing and enter my bedroom.

Next, I am lying in my bed asleep when suddenly I am awoken by the bed being lifted from the floor and flung violently from side to side. A great cave has opened up behind the headboard and all manner of night creatures are clamouring and swooping within its depths. Then there is a fearful squealing noise and I look down and the blue guitar case is opening and the little girl is getting out. She isn't dead after all, and is standing, looking out of the window. She starts to turn and at once I know it is going to be Kursty's face, but instead of a nose she has a bullet hole, with a flap of skin which opens and closes as she breathes. She looks to me and smiles, and a great wave of joy floods over me, and I cry and hold her bony, emaciated body in my arms.

'I wouldn't hurt you, Kursty, I love you,' I speak. She wets her lips and kisses me.

'You're dying,' she says.

I kick out my legs and shout 'no!' dragging myself from the floor.

'William Loveday is cold,' I tell myself, 'he must get dry.'

I shrug my jacket off my shoulders and rip my shirt off, the buttons pinging to the floor. I stamp my way out of my sodden trousers, pull the cover off the bed and clasp it to my shuddering body. I pick up my little candle and hobble out across the landing and down the stairs. Hideous shadows flare up all around me, and I swear by the devil that I mustn't come across my mother's laughing corpse.

I cross the hallway to the kitchen and crash my shins against a heavy piece of wooden furniture that shouldn't be there. I hop on one foot and kick at it on purpose, then cringe back fearfully. It really must be my mother's coffin. I hit the wall with my fist and, cursing, limp over and examine it under the light of my candle. It is a large wooden chest with my grandfather's name stencilled rudely across its lid. I clamber up on top and there's an envelope stuck there with my father's name typed on it:

For the attention of Mr W C Loveday
As the sole executor of the will of the late Charlie Loveday, Able Seaman, formerly of St Mary's Road, Gillingham in the County of Kent, it is my duty, in accordance with his last wishes, to place into your sole possession his Navy chest and contents as listed. Viz:
2 sets of 'fore and aft rig' including
1 'tiddly suit'
1 'milk-churn' hat, size 7/ + cap tallies
1 lanyard
2 pairs of Naval bellbottoms
2 jumpers, ditto
3 pairs of fisherman's woollen socks
2 pairs of combinations
1 duffel coat and kit-bag
1 'ditty-box' containing assorted service medals and insignia:
1914–15 Star
Great War medal
Victory medal
Long service good conduct medal
Second World War medal
Defence medal
1939–45 Star
and
1 bosun's whistle
1 brass telescope
1 tin of chocolate (Christmas 1914 issue)

Apparently my grandfather is dead. I jump down off the chest and crank it open with my scuffed hands, pulling out the contents and flinging them across the floor. Then I see a tin glittering in the folds of one of the jumpers! Cackling like a madman I bite the lid off with my bare teeth and I grin down at the little cube of mummified chocolate. I nurse it to my breast and kiss it, then scoff it into my face, chomping clean through the silver paper. It tastes bitter and musty, like sweet black dust. I fling down the empty tin and start ravenously sorting through the rest of the junk. A dark smell of old tar and mothballs comes up to me. An ancient pair of combinations . . . I climb into them and button them clean up to my throat.

Actually, the harsh wool chafes against my delicate skin, but I immediately begin to feel the benefit of their warmth. His milk-churn hat fits, everything! Only the bellbottoms are a little on the short side. I stuff two pairs of socks on, snatch up the kit-bag and take the candle with me into the kitchen.

When I open the fridge door, the stench of rotting flesh fills my nostrils, I gag and slam it shut.

I take the corner of my sailor's collar and suck on it for comfort. I check in all the cupboards. Dog food, dog food and dog food. By way of variation, I find a tin of cat food under the sink, and a rusty tin-opener.

There's a new box of matches and some candles in the drawer by the bread bin. I light all six of them and place them in a row above the sink. The effect is as if you just walked into a Russian church. Fairy lights flare up across the whole room, the taps glint as if golden candelabra, and are reflected again and again in the mirrors and glass, and I become more and more excited as I dance around the kitchen rifling through the contents of that strange and magical chamber.

On the bookshelf I find some tinned orange segments and a packet of instant custard powder. I eat the custard powder at once, then load everything else edible into my kit-bag.

I go back out into the hallway and stuff my feet back into my wet, busted shoes. I have one last peek into the bottom of the chest. Right at the bottom, nestling in the farthest corner, I find his moth-eaten old duffel coat. Beneath that is a little package containing my grandfather's medals. I feel their coldness in my hand then carefully pin them to my chest.

I hold the candle above my head and peer at my hideous looking face in the mirror. I am wearing my dead grandfather's clothes and will probably meet his ghost on the street and he will strip me naked and leave me to freeze to death. I truly believe this to be possible, and in fact it seems to me to be the most likely outcome.

All set to go. I sling my booty over my shoulder, lift the door latch and peer out into that frozen world. The wind snatches the handle from my grasp and hurtles into the house, shaking all of the furnishings and fittings. The old gas lamp in the kitchen swings off its hook and crashes down onto the kitchen table with a terrible smashing of glass. I jump back in fear, then, clasping my kit-bag tightly in my mitts, step out into that strange white world, dragging the door shut behind me.

No sooner have I stepped foot outside than low moaning rises up from within the smashed coach-work of my father's car. Evidently some large wounded animal has become entrapped in the wreckage and is now moronically bashing its grotesque head against the walls of its prison.

I walk past it on tip-toe. I am just clear when suddenly a cloud of snow goes up as the door is kicked open. It swings there drunkenly on its hinges. I stand giggling, tears biting at my chapped cheeks. There is a hurried scrambling, then a small shrivelled figure pulls itself from the wreckage and hops down onto the snow, swearing to itself. Seeing me, it lets out a low howl, followed by a quiet, malevolent chuckle.

'What have we got here then, burglars?' It fixes me with its impertinent eyes and takes two sharp steps towards me.

The spit dries in my mouth and I back away against the front of the house.

'Leave me alone!' I gasp, gripping hold of my kit-bag, ready to smash it into its disgusting face. I see that it is trying to entrap me by the chimney-breast and I break into a run across the snow-covered lawn. Immediately the spirits of the night are upon me, its dark figure scurries after me across the snow drifts and grasps me around the middle.

I have to decide whether to allow it to catch me or to run for my life. I sob and carry on running, dragging it along behind me. I wrestle with it, pleading with it to please leave me be.

It is Bernard, my father's taxi driver. I recognise the top of his head. I try to bite him, but he wriggles free.

He cocks his head and looks up at me.

'Is that you, master William?' he speaks. 'I'm sorry sir. I thought you might be thieves. Are you looking for your father, sir?'

I say nothing, pick up my kit-bag and brush off the snow.

'You couldn't spare us some change, could you, governor? The price of a cup of tea?'

I stare at this vile apparition before me. He blinks and steps towards me through the snow.

'That is you, isn't it, master William? I'm sorry, sir, I never recognised you, good evening, sir . . . are you looking for your father, sir?'

I nod at him, spellbound.

'You know me, sir. You know who I am?'

I shake my head.

'Why, I'm Bernard sir, your father's driver . . . What have you got in that sack, sir . . . You ain't got any grub in there, have you, guv'? . . .'

I tighten my hold on my kit-bag.

'Don't frighten yourself, sir . . . me and your father have had a little, er . . . falling out, so to speak, that's all . . . I'm not working for him anymore now, guv' . . . I'm down and out and destitute.'

He lowers his head to his chest and gives me a most cunning look. I shift my gaze from his weasely face to the wreck of my father's car.

'I know what you're thinking, sir, but it's not what it looks like at all, sir. That –' he points to the wreck, 'would never have happened if Bernard had been behind the wheel, sir.' Surreptitiously, and without warning, he draws himself right up to my face, his eyes glittering in his mask of yellow skin. 'Between you and me sir, we all know what your father's like, don't we, sir? We all know that he's partial to a wee dram and a fat whore! A small scotch and a slut! If you get my drift, sir?'

He winks one of his oysters at me.

'Not that I'd begrudge a man a drink, sir. Oh no, far from it, sir . . . your old man's the best employer I ever had, sir, a real gentleman he is, sir, a real gentleman.'

He leans in under my hat and in a hot whisper tells me that the police have been round twice in the week with a warrant for my father's arrest. I look at the oil stain in the snow and nod.

'Are you going away to sea, sir?'

I look at him questioningly.

'Your uniform, sir.'

I stare down at myself.

'To sea? . . . Yes, that's right . . . to sea . . .' I say thoughtfully. 'Yes, I ought to be getting along, my ship sails tonight.'

'You'll be going to join your family, sir?'

'Yes,' I say absently, staring at the wreck of my father's car.

'It's a terrible shame that, sir, isn't it?'

'Do you live in that car?' I ask him.

'Only for the present, sir. Until such time as I find myself another position . . . your father doesn't know I'm here, sir, so you'll pardon me, sir, for asking you not to grass me up, if you would be so kind, guv.'

'Where is he?'

'Your father, sir? I thought you knew, sir. You don't know where your own father is?' He looms in at me out of the dark and I have to resist the urge to push him into a snow-drift.

'No,' I say at last, 'I don't know.'

'Well, stone me, he's on holiday, guv', with his good wife, sir.

In the island paradise of Bali . . . it's in the South Seas I believe, sir. I thought you was sailing out to see them, sir?'

He nods at my uniform, wipes his mouth, rubs his oily hands together and looks hungrily at my kit-bag.

So, it is true, I say to myself. I have no family at all. My parents sun their repulsive bodies in paradise whilst their starving son crawls the streets of Chatham, half frozen, wearing the hand-me-downs of a dead generation.

'Would you like a tin of peaches?' I ask him.

He nods dumbly.

'No, sir! Thank you very much, sir.' He puts out his hand any-way. I stick my arm into the sack and pull out an unmarked tin.

'Oh, thank you, guv'! I ain't had a bite since yesterday afternoon, sir!'

A strange dream-like quality comes over me, as if I am hearing this nauseating little man calling out to me from across the infinite blackness of space, his mouth moving silently up and down as he does a little mime with his hands.

'Have you got a tin opener, guv?'

I grimace at him, turn on my heels and march round to the back of the house. I hear little Bernard scampering at my heels.

There is a push-bike leant up against the conservatory window. I walk over and pull it out of the snowdrift by its handle bars.

'You can't take that bike, guv', that's my daughter's bike that is, sir! I should never have borrowed it in the first place guv', my wife will kill me! It isn't mine, sir, it's my daughter's!'

I heave it out of the snowdrift, straddle the seat and smile down at him. I balance the kit-bag on the cross bar, stick in my hand and give Bernard the tin-opener.

'Goodbye,' I say, and standing on the pedals I wobble off into the snow.

It's like trying to pedal through sand. Little Bernard running along behind me, beside himself with grief.

'Please, master William, it's my daughter's bike, sir! My wife will never forgive me, sir. I'm destitute, sir, destitute!'

I lurch on up the alleyway and out onto the Walderslade Road. Immediately the wind hits me, the blizzard cutting in behind me, pushing me along ever faster, trundling along in the tyre tracks of a lorry. My grandfather's medals clank on my chest like saucepans. Bernard, made smaller by distance, stands with his hands fluttering at his throat.

I stand in the saddle and the wheels slither across the ice like snakes. Just as I hit the top of Waterworks Hill my bellbottoms, flailing in the wind like banners, catch in the chain and I'm chucked clean over the handlebars, one of them rising up and smashing me viciously in the solar plexus.

I lie winded in the road, gasping for breath. After twelve and a half seconds I pull myself to my feet. The kit-bag has split and the tins lie scattered across the snow-covered road. I kick them into the bushes then turn around and stand up the bike.

Over the brow of the hill lies the whole valley buried in deep silent snow. Occasionally, recognizable objects can be made out in between the mad flurries of the blizzard: a spindly tree, or the roof of an abandoned car, poking forlornly out of a treacherous drift. Footprints of night-cats stretch away into that invisible sea, to that magical place of endings and beginnings.

'Truly, I have no family!' I spit and there is blood in the snow. A tear wells up in my eye. Really, my eyes are streaming. I lift the bike painfully up onto my poor shoulders and step fearfully into that blinding whiteness.

Here our story ends.

APPENDIX
HERE STARTS THE NOTEBOOK INSCRIBED
BOOK THE 3RD

The ferry lumbers through the German sea. Every time we rise and fall there is a terrible boom as we hit the next great wave, every one of which seems intent on capsizing us. I awake face down on the floor.

The first thing I become aware of is that I am warm, lying under a table, and the floor is throbbing and juddering. My cheek rolls against the cold toecap of somebody's boot. The whole world shudders, the engines whining as the bow of the ship labours clear of the water and then smashes down again into the next great wall of water.

Voices above me cackle and explode into laughter. I hear the beer tipping down their open necks in great gulps, and then a cheer as someone gets up and accidentally stands on my nose.

'Come on, sailor boy, time to get up! Show a leg! Hands off cocks, hands on socks! It's eight bells, your watch! Tee, hee, hee!'

They are really having a ball at my expense.

'Come on, cabin boy! Get your trousers down, it's your shout!'

I pull myself from the floor, my anklebones cracking like pistol shots, and straighten out my uniform.

'Where'd you get all your gongs? You been in the war?'

Their leader screams with laughter at his joke and elbows his mates into a mooing agreement.

'You been in a war?' he repeats, then fills his face up with air till it explodes into a great raspberry and he falls to the floor clutching at himself.

I look down at my medals and give them a little polish with my cuff.

'They're me granddad's,' I explain. 'I'm wearing them in honour of his death.'

I can feel the weight of what I'm saying and a little lump comes into my throat and my bottom lip begins to tremble.

My tormentors look to each other, embarrassed. The old bald one picks himself up from the floor, sits down on his seat and peers into his empty beer glass.

'All right, calm down, for fuck's sake! We didn't mean anything, did we lads?' He speaks to me but refuses to look at me; instead he turns to his mate and addresses him.

'Has your granddad been dead long?'

'He died last week,' I say. 'He was blown into the water at Zeebrugge in 1918.'

They look to each other again and raise their eyebrows and the table grows silent.

'1918 wasn't last week,' says one of the subordinates, but the bald boss doesn't think it's funny enough so no one laughs.

They look like a little group of over-fed monks sitting there, staring into their empty glasses, waiting to have their bowls filled with gruel.

The ship rolls into a trough and a huge wave crashes down, knocking us broadside on. I go staggering across the bar; the bottles, the glasses, the tables and chairs – everything gets chucked against the wall and smashed down into matchwood.

We try to pick ourselves up, then another wave pours down on top of us. The engines scream and cough, struggling to bring us round. The old sea dogs look to each other and howl with glee.

'Bugger me, that was a big one!'

'I thought that was it!'

'The captain's pissed, I tell you – the old fool's been at the bottle and nearly sent the lot of us to Davy Jones's locker!'

They grin at each other, pleased as punch. Slowly we pull ourselves out of that pit and come round head on to smash into the next wave. The steward sticks his head over the bar and everybody gets a free mug of grog.

Righting the table and picking up their chairs, those old rascals offer me a seat. Really, I would much rather retreat back under the table and rest my emaciated body, but I sit and drink with them; out of politeness and fear, actually.

My belly revolts at the scorching rum, but I smile and swallow the sick as it comes into my mouth. The old bald one leers at me, his head glistening and a bright-red pair of side-whiskers sticking out like two ornate hedges. He pokes me in the ribs and laughs in my face.

'Go on, down in one, boy! That'll settle your stomach for you, or settle your hash. Har, har, har!'

No matter what your upbringing, it really was impossible to remain friends with a bunch of cutthroats like that.

'You're looking a bit pale, ain'tcha son? You ain't had too much to drink, 'ave you?' He winks broadly around the table. 'No, you've been too busy pulling your pud all night, 'aven't you?' He elbows his mates into laughter. One of them, a fat serious one, refuses, but baldy laughs right into his mug until at last even he has to open his fat gob and piss himself.

A blue blush comes to my white cheeks and I stare down into my grog.

'I reckon he has, boys, judging by the rings under his eyes. I'd say he's a regular little jostler, ain'tcha? Have you been polishing your Chinaman?'

He pokes at me with his prehistoric fingers, and the bow of the ferry drops and thunders into another mountainous wave. I hiccup, my ears burning painfully. The vile old cunt makes a fist of his hand and pounds away on the underside of the table, sticks his tongue out and bulges his eyes.

'Aye lads, he's a bit of a tosser all right!'

I sit there trying to laugh it off, stung to the quick by the utterances of this spindly old man who sits there wriggling his bristling red eyebrows at me like a monkey in a sideshow. Can it really be possible that this old polecat can read my most hidden and vile secrets, just by peering into the lines of my face?

'He's a little wanker, you mark my words, lads!' He shouts it out to the rest of the bar. 'That's why there's fuck all to him – he's wanked himself dry!' And he explodes into laughter again.

I look to my wretched pale hands and try to slap some blood into them. Could it be that quite by chance, on one of the swashbuckling adventures of his youth, this malevolent old bastard really had come into possession of a mind mirror?

He looks straight back at me and winks mischievously, as if egging me on in my ridiculous hypothesis. Had he then, in some exotic far-off land, met a South Seas witch who, cunningly disguising herself as a beautiful island maiden, had managed to seduce this boy sailor into selling his soul in exchange for this dubious, and possibly fictitious, mind mirror of hers? And, for all he knew, it might be a fake. After all, who says that there must be a mind mirror? On whose questionable authority was he acting?

I sit there dreaming up all manner of outlandish fairytales, only managing to confuse myself still further. A bottle of rum appears and a young writer's head becomes quite foggy.

I lean over the rail and let it go in hot rasping jets, my eyes stinging in that grey oppressive time before dawn.

The shoreline of an unknown land shows slate grey on the horizon and I shiver inside. A wave of grief seizes me and tells me to throw myself to the black, salty waves.

'Where is your loved one now, fool?'

I shake my aching head, tears springing to my eyes.

'In the arms of another,' I say gloatingly, goading myself with this pointed stick.

I sleep on the deck, flat out on my back, which is the only way I can keep from chucking up. I shiver and shake, the air so cold that it makes my fillings ache; my very bones turned cold as iron.

When I next look up we are passing some men on a barge that is so low in the water it looks like it's sunk. There is a lady on the back deck polishing a car and then one of the men steps up behind her and fondles her breasts as the others laugh.

On either side we are flanked by banks of black mud; we pass river traffic and the beginnings of cranes and industry. Sleek, oiled cormorants sit like black-cloaked sentinels on the rotting jetties and rusting buoys revolve in our muddy wake as we speed ever onwards towards the heart of this German nation.

Just then the man with the ginger whiskers comes out on deck and shoos me away from his mooring ropes, which I had been using as my bed. Shortly the whole deck comes alive and starts swarming with little men rushing from one end of the boat to the other, as a man in a grey duffel coat shouts at them through a loudhailer.

All those cranes must mean we are here. I stare down over the edge as the water gets more and more squeezed between us and the dockside, churning up into a black soup, covered in great oily bubbles. Soon it will be possible to reach out and touch the toy cranes on the dock. Ropes fly through the air and I am made to stand back from the rail. There is an almighty boom as we slam into a giant wooden fender. The man in the duffel coat shouts at me, but really it is not my responsibility.

They get that old tub lashed to the quayside and I have to go and collect my bike from the hold. Somehow, during the storm I should imagine, both of my tyres have gone flat. I look around for someone to say goodbye to, but there is no one. There is a doorway in the side of the boat and I freewheel my bicycle down the gangplank. There are some faces below me but not one of them says hello.

I pick my way along the quayside. No one has come to welcome me to this strange country of theirs. In fact they smirk at me and, on the whole, the welcoming party ashore is as rude about my appearance as were my shipmates aboard the ferry.

A man in a peaked cap and black leather gloves spits at me in his guttural tongue and waves his ape-like fists under my nose, before confiscating my new bicycle. Apparently I had been pushing it on the wrong side of the road. The Kapitain takes my bike by the handlebars and wheels it into a big shed. I run along beside him trying to explain to him, but he keeps his head down.

'It's mine,' I tell him. I mime riding it in front of him, even ringing the little bell, but he just holds me with his cold gaze, shakes his head and marches on. When we get into the shed he parks my bicycle up against the wall and orders me into his office.

Actually, he pushes me into a small room and locks the door on me. I call after him but can already hear his footsteps receding. I am forced to wait here alone in this windowless hut. There is a small birdcage stood on a pile of newspapers but there is no bird in it. The bottom of the cage is quite rusty and the door of the cage has been snapped off.

Really, this is not an office at all, but more of an old store cupboard. There are piles of moth-eaten files strewn about the floor and out-of-date phone books stacked to the walls. I am just examining the broken door to the birdcage when the door opens again and a very small man comes in.

This one doesn't speak any English either. He motions for me to roll up my sleeves, holds my arm in his girl-like hands, then peers through his little glasses, studying the thick blue vein that throbs in the crook of my arm.

'Opium?' he says thickly, and looks at me.

I shrug my shoulders.

'Morphine?' he asks me.

I shake my head. There is nowhere to sit in this dump and I have to stand. The truth is that he is stroking my delicate white forearms and trying to smile at me. He leans his small body against me and starts breathing in a strange way. I step backwards and knock over the empty birdcage. My new friend is pursing his lips in a most disgusting manner when there is a loud banging on the door and the man who stole my bicycle comes in to throw me out.

He leads me back along the quayside to a very large office building. We have to go back past the ferry, which is now quite empty and deserted. Everybody else has been allowed to pass unhindered and carry on with their journeys; it is only me who has been singled out to be harassed and humiliated by these stern officials.

There are a lot more men in the new building, dressed exactly the same as my officer, even to the extent of wearing the same moustache.

The Kapitain motions me to stand by a large oaken desk and a whole gang of his rough friends come over, crowd round and watch as he makes me sign a piece of paper which is covered in foreign words that I don't understand.

He draws a cross at the bottom of the page and motions for me to sign there by tapping it with one of his leather-clad fingers.

I take the stub of my pencil and sign it most carefully with my latest signature. He peers suspiciously at it, licks his lips, then takes a rubber stamp from out of the drawer and pounds it all over the newly signed document in quick, violent bounds.

His companions all nod to each other, congratulating him on stealing my bicycle. I smile quite fearfully at his blond moustache and pale eyes, but it is obvious that he doesn't like being looked at.

'I need my bicycle.' I try to reason with him but he refuses to listen. 'You see, it isn't strictly mine. It belongs to someone else. Another man ... Well, to his daughter, actually.' I do my best to explain but no one is listening. They all pour themselves a little drink and toast me, smiling, then show me the door.

Who are these people of the German nation? One thing is for certain – they have no care for the fortunes of a penniless young writer, which goes to show after all that the poor are indeed a worldwide brotherhood.

I look back at the dark ship and walk off alone, picking my way between the mooring ropes and old packing cases that litter their extraordinary dock-front.

All morning I sit on a pile of old tyres trying to make friends with one of their mangy dockyard cats. There is a black and white one who has a little 'Hitler' moustache under its pink nose and piercing yellow eyes. It sits on a pile of rotting timbers, not seven feet away, timidly looking at me. I try to coax it by rubbing my fingers together and singing 'kitty-kitty-kitty', but still it refuses to come to me. I go to stand and the idiotic cat immediately tenses its whole body and gets ready to scarper off down the side of the warehouse. I sit down again and, after a couple of minutes, the Nazi cat relaxes and starts to wash its face and ears. Suddenly I jump to attention and salute it.

'What are your orders, *mein führer?*'

The cat leaps from its pile of rotting timbers as if someone has stuffed a lit firework up its arse. When the cat hits the ground, it turns and glares back over its shoulder at me with such a look of hatred that I really feel sorry for my actions and try to call it back. I watch its tail disappearing for good down the side of the warehouse, dust my hands and really have to stifle a laugh. These German cats aren't nearly as fearless as they might have you believe.

At my feet is a dead fish. I toe it with my broken shoe; it seems that it was once a mackerel. I have no money and am beginning to starve. From across the river a large seagull flies up and comes to look at me. It circles round twice then lands on the deck and hops towards me. It isn't in the least bit afraid and is, in fact, quite bold and aggressive. It comes to a halt about five paces away and looks at me most malevolently. Apparently, it wants to eat the stinking fish that lies at my feet. I smile at the seagull sarcastically and then crush the fish's head beneath my triumphant heel.

'Neither cat, fish nor stupid fowl will get the better of William Loveday!' I shout.

I stare back at the seagull, daring it to come within striking distance. The seagull hops towards me again, making a barking noise. It flaps its large wings until I have to retreat round the back of my pile of tyres. I peer over the top at this ugly bird as it leaps upon the trodden fish and starts to devour it whole, its great hooked beak pulling out the fish's guts in one go, then guzzling them back, its throat bulging hideously.

There is a piece of packing case lying on the ground with a bent nail sticking out of it. I pick it up and weigh it in my fist. Just then, a man in bright yellow oilskins comes out from behind a huge stack of oil drums – about a hundred yards away – crosses his arms and stares at me pointedly, as if daring me to kill his vile, pet seagull.

I smile and wave at him but his face is expressionless. It is obvious that he has been trained not to respond in any human way to people who say hello. It really is as if he believes I have travelled all the way from England for the express purposes of stealing a piece of broken packing case. Carefully I put the piece of wood back down in the exact same place where I had found it.

I smile at him again, to show that no harm was intended, then start to slowly walk away. I look back over my shoulder and he carries on watching me most intently, following my every move with his German eyes.

Walking along like that, I trip and fall over a mooring rope ... which could be quite dangerous. I sit on the ground rubbing my ankle and peep over the edge of the quayside. The black river is there like a terrible darkness. I wish now that I hadn't put my club back, so that I could chuck it into the churning depths. I seriously consider going back to retrieve it, but the man in the yellow oil skins is still stood there. In fact he has climbed up on top of one of his oil drums, so he can get a better view of me. He shades his eyes and peers suspiciously at me from along the wharf.

I sit there raging against him. That man obviously thinks that he has won some great victory by forcing me to fall over against my will and robbing me of my ammunition. I look for a pebble or an old bolt to sling in the river, but there is absolutely nothing that isn't glued down. Too many times already today I have been humiliated and made a laughing stock by the people and wildlife of this foreign land.

I stare back at him and console myself by pointing out that he is, after all, only a German. Really just a dockyard rat, and that I, on the other hand, am William Loveday, and destined for greatness.

I'm going to take you around Hamburg – not the city, the docks. Commerce and romance: in that respect Hamburg's got something to look at. The day dies and a little mousy-mousy puts his whiskers outside his hole. It's time to take a gander around, to see what the tide's washed up. You see, a town isn't a town until nighttime. That's when it will reveal itself to you, slowly. Its true heart. That's when it's not too shy to show you its dirt.

It comes off the Elbe, that wind. A northern blast. Something you don't forget in a hurry. It pricks you with its sharp little teeth and finds your ribs. And the orange-faced whore at her lamppost, it's only half four and already her night begins to fall. A dull light, kind of diffused, like a piss stain spreading across the filthy sky.

The river is a strange place where husky men dip their hoary arms into briny barrels and swallow pickled herrings whole . . . The black water, in big stretches. I have to lower my head like a cow in a gale and arrange my collar around my chilblained ears.

It pulls you along, you become entangled, the quayside and all that water: black, foreboding. Little waves and wavelets competing. The lowest thing on earth: water . . . Then some blown-out factories, closed up and flooded . . . bakeries, wood-yards, iron sheeting . . . Cranes rise up and surround me, lit by a ghastly glow. Bridges, landing stages, girders woven into a latticework, as pretty as a maiden's plait. Industrialism from a bygone age; that always adds something, and a skyscraper full tilt, heading out to sea, not ship-like in the least. Containers mostly . . . fish, bananas and people. You see it all from the bridges; black, interwoven, impossible arcs through the sky, dreams . . . the water's edge.

A man with a hare-lip smiles kindly at me and I want to thank him, to climb up onto his wonderful crane and to polish its brass hook for him until it gleams like the sun, and he will know that I am worthy of his brotherly compassion.

Up a cheerless cobbled street I find a giant air vent puking out fumes; a grid this size! More like a tunnel . . . straight out at street level: a beer factory. It hits you right in the mug like an alcoholic's burp, warm and sticky. That's the yeast . . . dead beer and cigarettes . . . the remains of a bratwurst.

I hold onto the grid with my white fingers. 'Please, Kursty, somewhere in this town there is a woman waiting for me, to hold me and to love me. To feed me her milk-heavy breasts and caress my aching body. But just because this so-called woman loves me, it doesn't necessarily mean that I will allow her to lay her stinking flanks against mine. Or for her to touch me with her disgusting perfumed hands, for that matter. And I will, if I so choose, take my love and throw it down a bottomless well!'

A gang of sailors come past and laugh at me.

Am I not an Englishman? Only when compared to a German. But that doesn't make me necessarily a Swede either, does it? If anything it makes me a Russian with a black beard, but certainly not a figure of fun.

I stare into the black mouth of that vent. 'Kursty, come to me now. By magic, across the sea.' I listen out intently for her answer over the whirring of the ventilation shaft.

A police car passes and I have to hide behind a low wall. I peek out – a whole cavalcade of cars is swarming down the hill, blowing their horns at the girls stood there in their white, calf-length boots. The cars go in a big circuit. They merge and reappear, red tail-lights, then white headlamps. They do a little loop-de-loop then come back up the cobbled street and onto the main *strasse*.

I walk on, beneath a busted window. A girl waves and giggles. Shadowy, white-faced, a limb showing through the gloom, a bit of leg, then – *kerrboom!* An angel flare goes off and the whole scene is illuminated. I dash off, down a side street, it follows me, revolving on its little parachute, slantwise then – *phut!* It drops and fizzles out into the black river.

You see, I think I see something, then the whole picture dissolves. I have to remember it, to make sure that I really do exist, to remind myself that I really am alive, never to let anything die ever again.

In the grey morning light I stop outside a window display of disgusting bubbling meats. It appears that the Germans will eat all manner of sheep's eyes and offal. Above, a roast chicken looks down at me mockingly from its spit, then revolves sarcastically round and around in circles with five of its headless brothers and sisters. A man in a grease-spattered apron watches them dancing then turns to stare at me with such a look of malice in his fat eyes that I have to hurry away.

Actually, I have eaten a bar of chocolate which I stole out of the hand of a street urchin. His little face was so surprised that for several seconds he didn't even cry out but instead looked disbelievingly as I stuffed it, wrapper and all, into my munching gob.

Really, I am lying and didn't steal anything from any such person. But if the situation presents itself I will strike!

I cut down a back street, turn the corner and a man in a sailor's hat smiles at me with his skull face. I look down and straighten the medals on my chest. A doorway opens and I step in. When I look up I am in a den for all the lost and the smiling of hell: Die Geldern Handschuh.

To see such beauty there . . . I stand and stare at her across the pregnant, heaving mass of the room, through bitter cigar smoke and a cloud of cackling voices. 'Kursty,' I breathe. And it is really her, or at least her Norwegian cousin.

A lady screams; there's a punch and a glass falls and breaks. I stand transfixed and watch my beauty's eyes and feel my heart flutter under the skin of my chest. I will her to look at me but she won't.

I make my way to the bar, smiling round at those who surround me. I try to attract the attention of the landlady but she resolutely ignores me. Her gargantuan breasts loom at me as she sways past carrying trays of silly glasses of froth. Finally she looks up and questions me with her small, button eyes.

'*Ja*?' she shrills.

'Schnapps!' I answer, in perfect German, and she laughs in my face.

'*Nein*!' she squeaks and turns away. She picks up a tray of the little beers and really is going to leave me. Apparently, I was supposed to ask for Korn.

'Korn,' I say hurriedly and she 'tut-tut's me, puts down her

tray and really pours me one. She fills it right up to the top and places it in front of me. I knock it back in one and motion for her to fill the glass again. I clasp my iced Korn in my miserable fist and knock it back viciously. I hold onto the bar and smile round at those who surround me, but no one looks back at me or gives me that which I most crave: acknowledgement of my existence.

'If no one sees me, do I exist?'

The fat landlady pulls a leather purse from her apron. Now I have to pay for it. I show her my empty pockets.

'*Scheisse*!' she shouts and the room grows hushed. She shouts something else incomprehensible and a dwarf with a red beard steps menacingly towards me.

Quickly I unpin one of my grandfather's war medals and push it across the bar towards the fat landlady. It lies there in all the beer suds, the ribbon becoming quite wet. She looks disdainfully down at it, then gingerly picks it up and polishes it on her massive bosom. She looks me in the eyes then, baring her small sharp teeth, bites it. She smiles sarcastically, drops it into her leather purse and pours me another Korn. The dwarf steps back into the crowd and the conversation starts up again.

I swig at it and stand pointedly staring at the mysterious girl stood by the toilets, willing her to turn her head and notice me. She stands beautifully alone, studying her nails. She gives me a hard glance and then looks sharply away, as if I am boring her.

'You're wasting your time there, my friend.' A man in a silver cape leans into my ear, breathing heavily. His breath smells of garlic. 'She's not interested in the little pecker of an Englishman.'

I refuse to look at him. Every single cell of my being is drawn up, standing to attention and leaning towards the mysterious girl, stood by the toilet door. My intestines squirm like snakes, but not rudely. Before, I had almost felt normal but now my heart jumps in my chest in fear and anticipation. It is as if she is a dark star and I am to be sucked into her heart and dashed to smithereens.

The man in the silver cape nudges me in the ribs. I look down at his brown, bejewelled fingers and he laughs his gold teeth at me.

'You've spotted one there, my friend! My God, you should see your face. You would think that you were staring into a can of worms rather than at the breasts of beautiful woman!'

He takes a cigarette out of a gold case, lights it with a matching lighter and blows smoke up to the ceiling. 'Don't even bother thinking about it; she's got her legs stitched together, you mark my words!'

He has a small silver beard and two diamond studs on the collar of his cape.

'My name is The Sex Pope.' He does a little bow. I nod and finish my glass of Korn.

'You want another, I pay?'

I shake my head.

'Where do you come from in England?'

'I'm not English.' I lie.

'But you would like another drink?'

I can see that this silver buffoon is intent on keeping me indebted to him until all hell freezes over. I stare at the rows of funny coloured bottles behind the bar.

'I was robbed by ghosts,' I explain to him. 'Six of them! I suppose they were pirates, or even highwaymen.'

My friend with the silver cape smiles at me but I can detect something mocking in his whole demeanour. Obviously, he has been sitting here patiently waiting to pay for some poor down-and-out's drink so's he can get on his high horse and purposefully humiliate them.

'Are you in need of a little money, my friend?'

I shake my head

'Somewhere to sleep then, perhaps?'

This fool obviously thinks my situation highly amusing, because all the while he is smirking to himself and winking besottedly at each and every floozy in the place. Two Thai girls, stood close in behind him, cling to the hem of his cape with their tiny fists, staring up at him with cloying admiration.

I fumble for a cigarette but I don't have any. There is a half smoked dog end in the ashtray which I pick out, clean off and look about for somebody who's smoking. I really am intent on asking the girl who looks like Kursty for a light, but the man in the silver cape insists on lighting it for me with his expensive lighter.

I stare at her, puffing on the twisted cigarette, then I go into a coughing fit and this Sex Pope actually has the barefaced cheek to bang me on the back.

'There there, don't be so obstinate. Let me introduce you to my . . . little friends.'

He motions for the two Thai girls to step forward. They smile up at me out of their dark little faces but he doesn't tell me their names, instead he introduces himself all over again.

'The Sex Pope, at your service!' And he bows and the Thai girls just giggle. 'My card. If you require anything of me just ask and all will be delivered unto you, my friend.' And he winks at me. I have to look away.

'You can't take your eyes off that woman, can you?' and he nods towards the girl stood by the toilets. I look to her, still stood beautifully alone.

'Forget her, my friend, forget her! Take it from me, she isn't worth it. This is where it's at!' He pats his two Thai girls on their heads and they smile up at me like two small children.

'German women?' he spits. 'Danish women? Turkish women? They're all *scheisse*! They don't want to do it! They've got PMT! They want a pay rise! To hell with the lot of them! Give me Thai girls any day of the week!' He smashes his fist into the palm of his other hand for emphasis. 'Thai girls are the only ones for me. They might not show any enthusiasm, but by God they know how to take a cock!'

I look at my fingernails.

'You,' he says evenly, 'are an Englishman.'

I try to contradict him, but he raises his hand and shushes me as if he is my father, which he certainly is not.

'You are an Englishman,' he continues, 'and I am a Frenchman!' He bulges his hooded eyes at me. 'Certainly, the English are polite and gentlemanly but tell me, what would an Englishman know about the requirements of a woman? Nothing!' he spits, 'whereas I, my friend, was in the concentration camps and only escaped by the skin of my teeth! It takes cunning, it takes stealth, it takes endurance. How do you think I got out of that place? I fucked my way out, that's how! It takes a French cock to know how to really service a whore, to know her most intimate needs and requirements, to give her what she really wants!' And he bangs his fist down on the bar, almost spilling a lady's drink. He turns and smiles at her, patting his crotch.

This disgusting old Sex Pope lifts his cape and pulls his Thai girls in close to his French body.

'René, the French fuck machine! That's what those hot little bitches called me. These bastard Germans don't know the first thing about pleasing a woman!' He dismisses the entire male population of the German nation with one gesture of his hand.

'I'll show you what fucking is! When I started out I was the only stud in the whole of St Pauli. I worked flat out, seven nights a week, three-hundred and sixty-five days a year, plus a matinée on Sundays, for six consecutive seasons. My cock was so hot it used to singe the hairs on their arses! Germans? Englishmen? They can't even get it up; they don't know what a stiff cock looks like. You have to insert it for them – by hand. Soft cocks, I'm surrounded by soft cocks!' He slaps the Thai girls' flanks and pretends to chase them round the bar.

The crowd nods and encourages him with their eyes; they raise their glasses and shout obscenities. Then, all of a sudden, The Sex Pope claps his hands and yells that the fun is over. The girls look at him obediently. He reprimands them. One of them he calls Tina, and pulls her by the hair quite violently. The girls must compose themselves for tonight's show. He checks his watch and flays his cape.

'You, my friend –' and he points at me '– are most graciously welcome to visit my humble sex club!'

Then he turns and departs, the crowd swallows him, his silver cape shimmering in the darkness of the bar. He kisses his fingertips, rubs his balls and exits. He's needed elsewhere; he doesn't need to explain himself to me. In my mind I wish him to drop dead.

In all the commotion the girl by the toilet has left. I look desperately around the room for her face but she is gone.

I want to stay by the bar and look for her but I have nothing left to drink. Instead I go to the toilets and fill my glass at the dirty taps. I take a swig, look in the mirror and let it dribble back out down my chin. Then a man comes in and I have to pretend that I am washing my hands.

I wait till he leaves, pick up my glass and follow him back out into the bar. He has a leather coat on and seems to be dragging his left foot behind him, which I fancy is made out of tin. I decide that I too should have a tin leg and come out limping behind him. He turns abruptly and I have to cringe back in fear, in case he hits me.

The Norwegian Kursty is back, stood there by the door, and I have to make myself talk to her. I introduce myself and am very polite, but she refuses to speak to me. I tell her that my name is William Loveday – that I am a young writer down on my luck, and that I am stranded all alone in this harsh German town with nowhere to sleep, but she just snorts and turns away from me.

I stand there next to her for quite a long time, trying to think of something important to say. Finally I ask her if her name is Kursty, which she says it isn't. For someone so beautiful she really does speak rather poor English.

'My name is Janet. I go now.'

I smile as if this is good news.

'I don't believe your smile,' she says sharply.

And I laugh, but really I am very afraid of her and wonder if she really can see parts of me that I have hidden.

Then she really does smile at me. But actually, across the room, she has seen a man who has large forearms. It is the dwarf with the red beard who she is smiling at, not me.

I follow her gaze. The dwarf spits and turns from her. I can't believe that he can be so nonchalant when such a woman as this has just given him the benefit of her smile. He drinks his small beer in a rough way and flexes his forearms, which seem to be covered in a ridiculous layer of ginger fluff.

I am better than that man, Janet. It is for me only that you should smile, because one day soon I will be dead and you will cry for me then, Janet, and beg me to forgive you. I know this is true because I am your master, Janet. Because I am better and wiser than this man with ginger arms.

I drink my tap water in vicious gulps and put my hand in my pocket, grinning cunningly at my clever observation.

The legs of all the people in the bar rise up around me like a forest and I imagine that I am kissing Kursty's feet.

Janet, you are Kursty and I love you. Your flint-like eyes and the corners of your mouth: I want to curl up in there, to climb somehow into your mouth and dissolve my aloneness – this terrible dissolution that I carry like a banner on the street, that all can read in my hungry eyes, tolling the bell of my uncleanness. Take me and absorb me into every tingling cell of your body. No wonder I recognised such beauty, for in reality we carry the same banner, for we are brother and sister. Both of us broken and destroyed.

I crave the sensation of your touch, Janet. Just lay your eyes upon me and that will be like the kiss of any other woman. I have lost my heart before, you see, Janet. I took it out of its little blood box and it quivered with delight in the palm of that harlot who kissed it, pulled a sour face and then flung it to the dust. And now I pick it up from the dirt, spit on it, wipe it on my trouser leg – this poor piece of rancid offal – and offer it to you. Please hold it and caress it and don't torment me any more. Or better still, ignore me and look forever away, Janet. Yes, that's how to treat this shyster. You've got the measure of this fake smiler, Janet. This thief whose only wish is to soil your beauty; to drag you off your pedestal, push you down upon your knees and make you take him into your beautiful mouth in worship. You will bow to me and know me as your brother, sweet Janet. I come to you now in my broken shoes, dragging my soul through the grime.

I gibber in front of her and feel her holding me at arm's length with those impossible green eyes, slanting like beautiful daggers.

'If a beautiful woman walks into this room, you walk straight up to her and kiss her!' she speaks.

I look at her, my grin taut on my face. It is true, how well you read the depths and depravity of this stinking soul, Janet. I would stand to the arms of such a woman and bite at her lips till they bled. But in truth, I'd lack the one good, wholesome quality that you accuse me of possessing, and instead I'd stand dumb, paralysed in fear and self-doubt, as she walked past me and into the arms of another.

I can't pretend that my mind doesn't scream at all times with lust and disjointed fantasies . . . to stop the world and fuck all the girls . . . desperate to know myself, then recoiling in fear . . . my nose following the arses of unknown girls on unknown streets and every wank is a release for those few pitiful seconds before I must stand and race on again to blot out the next great sob of pain. An impossible breast swings before me, plump and heavy with milk, my lips puckering but never to succour my poor aching heart.

And so I reach for her . . . Janet leans away from me, lifts my hand that cups her small breast and drops it back onto the bar. The room swims around us and I see her as a child.

'How old are you, Kursty?'

'I tell you already, my name is Janet.'

'How old are you, Janet?'

Nineteen,' she speaks.

'Nineteen and a virgin?'

She looks away in pain, then turns again, her beautiful pink tongue just showing behind her beautiful lips and teeth that I could swallow.

'You like to talk like that, don't you? To say bad things.'

'When can I fuck you, Kursty?' I say her name wrong on purpose. And she falls silent. I scratch at a spot on the bar with my thumbnail.

One day, Janet, you will write me a letter, one day you will hold my hand. Only I might be dead by then, this street dissolved to dust. And you will cry for me then, Janet, and beg for me through your tears stinging your eyes, hating yourself, damning your very heart for having the temerity to have denied me.

'I like your broken shoe.' She points to my flapping sole.

Yes, everybody likes my flapping sole, because everybody loves art. Only they don't know what art is, and those who say they do are the biggest liars and scoundrels of them all!

I'm a bad boy and regret my big mouth, only I love myself for it also. I give myself special permission, above all others, to

love myself and speak the vilest rumours against myself. To teach myself a lesson I won't forget. To admonish myself for having these unnatural desires, for seeing the world through such base eyes, for daring to wank myself into oblivion.

I walk out of there clasping her address in my hand like gold. I sniff the scrap of paper for her scent. I kiss it and lick at the ink, but I refuse to eat it and instead fold it carefully into the depths of my pocket.

I cross the Reeperbahn and head off up Davidstrasse. I stand sheltering by the police station in the drizzle till early morning and that's where I see them – my shipmates from the voyage – sat behind the plate glass window of the Wienerwald like a bunch of wise monkeys.

A white knuckle raps on the window at me and I stare up into space. Then they all bang on the glass with their fists in unison and that's when I see them. One fellow sticks his fingers up at me, which is childish. Apparently I was walking along with my head in the clouds and looked plainly ridiculous.

A prostitute looks at me and I become excited and have to hunt around in my pockets. I walk back and forth on the pavement looking for the entrance to that dump, which takes me several minutes and gives them a whole new chance to mock me.

Finally, I duck inside and walk over to their table, my bellbottoms flapping like banners at my knees. As a matter of fact they take the rise out of my fancy dress all over again. The one with the red side-whiskers even peers into my face and says, 'Yuck, acne!' which stings me. He grins at me viciously, then looks down and sucks noisily on his glass of froth.

The disapproval of my shipmates hangs in the air like dense blue smoke. I understand now that all emotions have corresponding colours: green, for instance, is loathing and disrespect.

My chair scrapes noisily and hurts my toothache. It seems that they have decided to let me know, in no uncertain terms, that I am an outsider; that I don't belong and am not welcome at all. Which is unkind of them. It seems, after all, that the rules of the playground apply throughout life. I order myself not to be too friendly, not to creep and not let them know that they've hurt me.

I am immortal, I tell myself. I am a desperate man with desperate hands and feet.

'My cock,' I shout at myself, 'has blue veins and a humpty back.' I shout it in a language nobody else can understand, then stare down at the chequered floor.

I let myself slump over that Formica tabletop and dribble onto my cuff.

The Wienerwald: an eatery for the down-at-heel and poxy, directly opposite the police station. It's got *Polizei* written all over it in pretty blue letters. Those letters fix themselves to my eyes and the streets swarm with the lost. My heart hangs by a thread. I nibble despondently at my peeling lips and try to smile at my hostile companions.

Someone reads out the menu card in broken German and I
smirk to myself and pretend that I've just thought of something
incredibly funny, which I have. A kind lady puts a cup of tea
down in front of me and I smile after her as she walks away. I
stamp my feet and accidentally knock the leg of the table and
somebody tells me to 'Shut it!'

The crew makes their selections from the card and the pimps
and the whores, the school kids and the lost, the whole sad parade
just keeps grinding past the window. People we will never know
and will never see again, their delightful little ears, silly noses and
frightening eyes. I watch them all passing with sadness.

To bully everyone or to become a microscopic dot in some
miserable backwater? A judge or a thief? Either you buy and
you sell in this world or else you fuck off! And here they all
come, just look at that Caesar: the mug of ages, dealing and
selling – right down through the centuries – in blood and guts.
Jowls hanging beneath his ears like little nests of lard.

Whatever else you might say, you can't deny that it's only the fashions that change – it's the same ugly mug that rots in jail or swigs brandy from under a judge's wig.

The prostitutes huddle out there in the rain. The comings and goings of Diamond Lil'. Ten minutes pass and she pops up again. I peep out the window like a puppy dog, my clipped claws making little clattering noises at the window pane. She chews her gum with venom then glares at her diver's wrist watch till the hands curl.

She holds me with her tragedy, something reassuring in an ever-changing world, something immortal. And her mug painted to perfection, her nose smack bang in the middle of her face, exactly where it's supposed to be.

Of course, one day she goes off for a knee-trembler and never returns. You search for her in all of her old haunts, but this time she really has gone and turned up her toes. And what's even more sad is that you don't really miss her. The world turns and after a month or two you can't even recall her face. Just a shadow, an idea ... her lamppost empty, her daughter stood there in her mother's shoes, staggering around in a pair of her old stilettos; her knees knocking like a pair of castanets. Maybe we'll utter a few empty words, mumble a borrowed sentiment or two, before we turn, button our lips and trudge on to our own sorry little endings, our own engagements.

She leans back against her lamppost, spits her gum into the gutter and lights a cigarette. I remember you, my dear, and I wave to you in my mind.

If I had been born as a woman, and by nature I would make a perfectly good woman, I would dress exactly as I do now and walk up to unknown men on the street, kiss them savagely on the lips and then just turn and walk away. But they would still know that my kiss was a gift, and one that I hadn't given lightly.

And even if I preferred the company of women, I would still love men with a fierce loyalty. One thing is for sure, I would refuse to wear any makeup, except for maybe a smudge of kohl on my eyelids, and naturally I would tie my hair in a thick knot. All in all I would regard my body as a dagger that I would withdraw from its sheath, as and when I pleased, and hold it gleaming before the hungry eyes of deceitful men, who I would then let touch it only to see their fingers bleed.

I grow more and more excited by this strange and unexpected turn of my feverish mind and spoon ten heaped sugars into my tea and knock it back in quick, noisy gulps.

Naturally my body would be powerful and muscular and my breasts and buttocks would be oiled by the hands of virgins. I would dance like a black woman and paint my nipples cobalt blue. Of course, being a woman, it wouldn't necessarily follow that I would desire to be held and kissed by men at all. Even if at the bottom of my heart, disguised by fear and anger, lay a deep, yet lifeless sea of love and compassion waiting only for a brave prince to break into that innermost chamber and destroy the coiled dragon that lay gloating over my shivering soul.

Of course, for a woman, her body is her cock and for a man his cock is his body.

My shipmates finish their chicken and sit back picking at their teeth, which is common of them. I look down at their dirty plates and imagine licking at those bones.

Food is just another trick set to trap me. I watch them slapping their fat greasy chops together and have to jam my cuff in my mouth to stop myself from chucking up. Really, I just smile.

They order coffee and more beer.

'This stuff is shit! If we knew we were having chicken we should have gone to Shultze's chicken house. He knows how to fry that stuff!'

The table nods and moos in agreement. I try to catch their eyes, but they just look to each other and throw their napkins down in disgust. I'm left to clean the bones, hunt the remnants down and devour them. One day I will become a louse with a moustache, a scurrying bone-licking louse!

I look up and wipe my chops with my cuff. Diamond Lil' is back. She re-finds her lamppost, stands and beats her arms and thighs for warmth, the air fogging at her mouth. She looks up to my window and gives a little wave. I take my nose out of the greasy plates and smile through the remnants.

She tucks her arse in, then it's straight back to business. She hangs her leg out at a jaunty angle, taking up the whole pavement ... fiddles with her perm and casts her net ... a black widow with a web from here to hell. I tell myself that she's got eight eyes and a leg hooked round every thread. The longer it takes for her to find another client, the more excited I become.

In my dream I walk right up to her, stare into her star-blown eyes and tell her my poem. I read line after line to her until tears start to divebomb off her nose into that orange, puke-stained night, and she begs for me to stop. Next, her cold hand claws at my arm and, grizzling with pain, she leads me back through the night streets to her bed, where she breaks down before me and, wetting my thighs with her tears, begs me to forgive her sins, which I laughingly do. And so she hugs my loins and renounces her evil life forever.

No sooner is she back on her spot than she rustles up some hapless youth. She blows up his nose and strokes his zipper. Evidently she is not at all bashful. She grabs him by his tie and hauls him in, wriggling like a wet fish. He slithers across the pavement, slips out of her hands and plops back into the gutter. Lil' sticks in her arm, hooks him out again and he stands there spinning with a big 'Ooo!' on his lips.

She pulls out his pocket linings and counts out his loose change: two lousy Pfennigs, a bit of fluff and a gob-stopper.

He stares at her hopelessly, showing her his empty palms. Nothing, not a sausage! He's no punter, just a harmless youth wending his way home from class on a cold and freezing night ... his school satchel still slung over his shoulder. That makes her giggle.

She glances up to my window again and I fancy that she

looks very deeply into my eyes and winks at me. I try to smile back, then I look around to see if any of the others have noticed me. Some rough people in the cafe bang on the glass at her, egging her on and behaving like utter brutes.

A small crowd gathers; apparently they're on her side, which is disgraceful.

She rubs his pecker and ties him to the lamppost by his school tie. He shakes his head like a horse, but resistance is futile . . . her charms . . . a glint of fun in her eyes. She's got him beat, caught him walking on the cracks in the pavement and now he's hers.

She pouts and gurgles, tweaks his belly and purrs indecently. The school boy pleads with her, he goes limp and shows her his empty linings, but he definitely wants it, our Diamond Lil' can tell. An expert, never been wrong in fifteen years! Men? They're her business. She swallows them like flies and spits out the zippers!

Finally he nods in defeat and a little cheer goes up. She unties him, takes a curtsey and leads him away by his reins.

The crowd parts and lets her through, him in tow. I can just see her head . . . her perm glistening day-glow orange in the fairy lights . . . her arse encased in lycra . . . a sea of bodies, then they're gone . . . between the crowds of legs . . . bright lights . . . raised voices . . . into the night . . .

The crowd hangs in mid-air, lost in reverie. They stand around chewing the fat, still enchanted.

They remind themselves of what they've just seen and laugh all over again. They mime it out all in front of them. A man with a black moustache pretends to lead the boy away. His companions howl at him and he stands there, proud of his thick moustache. Something's happened, they're dead impressed, but now it's over.

Next up, I see the dwarf from The Golden Handshoe picking his way down the street. I watch his red beard, then he comes in through the glass door carrying his accordion. My shipmates greet him like an old friend. They slap each other's backs, everyone has a drink, then they get out their violins. There's lots of discussion about sea shanties. They're all going back over to The Handshoe for a knees-up. The dwarf turns to me and orders me to carry his accordion for him. I stoop and pick it up and they all march out. I tag along behind, carrying that thing.

'*Kan ich bit zahlen?*' I practise my German. The crew turns to look at me like I'm speaking double-Dutch, then dig out their wallets, pay-up and leave.

Max, Hamburg Agent No 1 – he fixes the gigs and passes round the beer tickets. I get lumped in with everyone else. It seems that they have to play four sets. The first one from half twelve till three, the second from half three till seven. That makes eight hours, or at least six. And what about breaks? They can talk about that later, first they have to get the instruments unloaded. I'm to pretend to play the triangle.

An old-time swing band is supporting the blue movies. The group is on stage and a screen is above their heads. That's what the tourists want: a cold beer and a spectacle! A cock in every orifice! They've come to get fucked and sucked, only they're not quite sure. First they want to sniff at it, to take just a tiny sip before they open their disgusting traps and down the whole stinking lot. To swallow it, to regurgitate it . . . they get a sour stomach . . . they drift in and they drift out . . . they're not sure . . . they're drunk . . . they're soused . . . they're stark raving bonkers!

I stand by the back entrance and watch the driver reversing the horse and cart. He battles with the reins. He gives the horse some terrible strokes with his whip. Finally the gee-gee starts backing up and he lets off the handbrake. The cart swings drunkenly across the road and he nearly smacks into the wall. And then there's an argument about who's strong enough to be able to get the back doors open.

I step in and shoulder the double bass, so that they will all see how strong I am; that I have chosen the heaviest instrument which normally takes two people to carry between them. Actually my shoulders are too narrow to balance it properly and my collar bone is quite badly bruised.

The one with red side-whiskers mocks me, then disappears into the toilet. He looks thoughtfully at the double bass and then happens to notice that his bladder is full. He fiddles with his cap, adjusting it several times upon his bald pate. He raises his hand as if to speak, then catches himself mid-utterance and snaps his fingers, like some forgetful nephew who, after returning from the shops on some errand or other for his bed-ridden aunt, suddenly remembers he has forgotten the one item that this stern invalid had impressed upon him to be sure never to forget, namely a small tin of pilchards.

Just in this way he snaps his fingers, about turns and disappears into the bowels of the building. I hear him swearing to himself as he goes. I lose him. I look for him but he's gone. The others will have to unload and set up without him. They can't find him? Fine, then they will have to set up by themselves.

Everything comes off the back of that old cart. Instruments of yesteryear, with a special sound. No public address system. No amplifiers. Just acoustics.

The driver checks the equipment off. I select a small box and bang in through the doors of the club. I stroke the horse's soft nose. He *clip-clops* his feet but I haven't any grub for him. I say goodbye, grab a suitcase and go back inside. I head straight for the little stage at the far end and fiddle busily with my triangle. I get it out of its case and bend their ears. I tune up. Really, the rust is this thick!

There is something wonderfully feminine about my hands, beautiful yet tragic; undoubtedly artistic, but prone to obstinacy. Untutored and full of themselves, totally unwilling to obey the simplest of orders. Or, if you like, laughing up their sleeves at me.

And then of course, there's my ears. I'm tone deaf. They picked me out as the class moron in school. 'Just mouth it,' they said, 'or sit down and shut up!'

I keep on tapping right up until they open the doors and let the audience in. My hands like great white butterflies. Then I have to quit it.

The ship's crew stands huddled by the bar. I walk over so as to have someone to stand with. Again, no one talks with me. Apparently, I have transgressed some new, unwritten law. I pretend not to be watching the pornography on the screens, and then I pretend that I'm thinking about my shoe. I go and peel a used piece of tape off the stage and wrap it round my broken sole.

A beautiful girl walks in through the swing doors and drapes her fur coat over the front of the stage. Some debutante waltzes in. Some pimp's whore with powder this thick! The one with red side-whiskers stops talking and watches her deposit her fur. Once her back is turned, he sidles up to the stage, jumps up and kicks her rag onto the floor. He boots it across the tiles – 'rat skin'! The girl runs, snatches it back up and pulls a face. Side-whiskers slaps his knees and laughs till he's sick. The girl's friend takes her arm and they both walk out to the ladies' room. Side-whiskers walks back to his mates, still laughing, and gulps down another beer. I watch through the open doors. The lady applies some more paint, checks in her mirror and draws circles . . . scarlet . . . she pouts.

These women aren't mine; I am like an angel. These women come and they go, flitting on the arms of their shiny new men, trying to lose themselves, to puke themselves out of their miserable heads. They stand in front of their mirrors, congratulating themselves. They order another bottle of Champagne. Champagne? *Elbe wasser*, my dears! Rat's urine, watered to piss! No, they have no time for a young writer, down on his luck, in a foreign town.

I *ding* and *ting* at my triangle. I draw blood . . . I play for them all, without discrimination . . . a lot of bum notes. The beautiful don't even notice; nobody cottons on. They're oblivious to everything but their cocks and their wallets.

Fifty songs we play that night. At least. Seventy even! From my heart and my busted nails ... I've still got the set list, preserved, to remind myself ... hidden somewhere safe ... lost ...

The night begins to fade and disappear and the band has to improvise, to pull songs out of thin air. The audience sways and hiccups. They boo and jeer. Someone passes me a ukulele. I have to try and tune it. Honestly, for fifteen solid minutes I work those machine heads, grinding the cogs through thirty years of rust and grime. Then just as I get it in perfect concert pitch two more strings bust at the same time, an 'A' and a 'G' I think. They ping off in a cloud of rust. After all my scrupulous efforts to hear all the harmonics, the subtler overtones ... and meanwhile the drummer is bashing ten types of shit out of his cymbals, right in my ear.

I throw my guitar down in disgust and walk out to the toilets. I order a beer.

'Einer grosser pills, bitter!'

The barman stares at me blankly. I have to give him a beer ticket. The doorman wants a pint as well.

'Make that *zwei*!' I yell at him.

'*Dumkopf*!' he mutters, scrapes the froth off with his knife and slings the glasses across the bar at me.

'*Danke schön*!' I shout.

'*Bitte*!' he yells and slams the beer down, almost spilling some.

I pick it up carefully and examine the counter for loose change. The barman gives me a meaningful look and I saunter off to find the doorman.

He is stood there at attention in the rain, his face completely tattooed. Great scrolls and flourishes are drawn right across both cheeks. Even his eyelids are biro-ed in and a ring clean through his nose. He likes trinkets, I can see that much ... a regular Queequeg. A man out of a picture book.

He narrows his eyes, takes the beer from my hand and sucks on it. He smiles, but still I feel I haven't done enough for him and rack my brains for some appropriate gift I can present him with. Suddenly I have an idea: I can give him a badge. There's one hanging loose from my sleeve, a couple of stripes just coming unpicked. I give them a tug; they rip and come free. I hand them to Queequeg. He stares down, his bottom lip hanging out, then a smile spreads out across his emblazoned mug.

'My grandfather's,' I explain.

'Grandfather!' he rumbles.

'That's right, Queequeg. He fought the Germans – at sea!'

Queequeg motions to me in sign language, then lifts his hand: *'Halt!'* He goes through his pockets. *'Ein moment!'* And he pulls a picture postcard of himself out of his back pocket and waves it through the dark air.

He mimes something in front of me. I watch him, his lips moving, but silently. He draws something in front of me in thin air. I think I follow him. A bird? . . . In flight? . . . With small wings! . . . With fire?

I nod and smile, feel for my stub of pencil and hand it to him. He has to use my shoulder as a rest; he licks at the lead and spits. He pulls a face and almost laughs.

'Mee Queequeg!' he rumbles as he writes. He labours over it, peering through the flashing lights. Then, straightening up, he hands it over to me: an old picture-postcard of himself stood in front of a Stuka. I hold it up to the light. Not bad!

'Thanks Queequeg, thanks a lot!'

'Mee fly. Over England!' He points to his picture and thumbs himself in the chest. *'Staffelführer.'*

I pat his shoulder, broad, tattooed. He doesn't say a thing, dumb as a horse. He motions; he emphasises with his hands. A man of very few words. He looks down at his badge.

'Grandfather.'

'That's right, Queequeg. He was at Jutland.' I make some explosion noises and he smiles.

Queequeg says who's getting in and who's staying out and that's that. A nod of the head, a jerk of the thumb, yes or no. He keeps out the riff-raff.

Of course, Queequeg's not there any more; he's gone and turned up his toes. Laid up in some hospital bed, dying of lung cancer by all accounts. A tattooed man. Tattooed from head to foot. Toes, fingers, nose, forehead, eyelids, the whole caboodle! Completely covered. Rings in both ears, his nose and his mouth, and a Mohican, dyed jet-black, with a ponytail right down the middle of his back! Oh yes, you'll recognise him all right . . . Queequeg, a man who doesn't go in for half measures. They'll be burying him soon.

The audience thins out, the night drawing to a close and no woman has come to rescue me.

I quit bashing my banjo and light up a foul cigarette. All in all the roof of my mouth is raw and burning. I spit and swig at the last of my beer, warm and gritty, just a drip in the bottom of the bottle. Everybody except for me puts on their coat and heads for the door. I stand there marooned, then shuffle after them enjoying the new pain that I have discovered in my foot.

I put my nose round the door – daylight! I gag on the air, peering through the beer fumes. Half seven . . . a little bird sitting on his perch . . . a busted sapling growing out the dog shit. He starts up singing, all by himself, bold as brass . . . forlorn . . . against all the odds, so to speak. Just like me.

I walk along listening out for his song. I try to spot him, dawdling along with my head in the bushes. The others are disappearing. I have to run to catch up.

On the way I see my floozy of the night before, still standing on her corner. I try to smile at her but she doesn't look in my direction, so I duck and walk on pretending that I have thought of a fine joke, one that I have been saving for myself all night.

So you're still on the game. An all-night worker, puts everyone else to shame. I say goodnight in my heart. I'm off to bed with myself, until this evening . . . to get some shuteye and breakfast, if anyone will feed me.

I have been sleeping in a derelict bomb shelter. Frost on the roof and no windows and no doors. A fox came in to visit me.

The last orders I received from the dwarf were to meet outside The Star Club at four in the afternoon to meet our contact. I have to look out for him.

Today I have given myself a secret message which I am not to disclose to anybody. It is to do with my being saved, which buoys my heart no end and makes me feel very special. I put on my milk churn hat and climb out of the escape hatch, cross over the road, left onto *Grosse Freiheit*, and then it's just half way up.

I bow my head under the lights, a million bulbs all busted and the grey clouds . . . that's impossible!

I see him, way off, gesticulating . . . a silver cape and gold teeth. He throws his little cane about like a magician, silver topped. He beats it on the pavement and surveys his domain. The orchestra stood obediently before him.

I have to hobble, to run and catch up with them. I put my limp on and arrive gasping in the entrance hall. Actually I force myself not to breathe and purposely put my full weight on my swollen foot.

Here he is again: The Sex Pope, in person, flighty as a blue tit. They have to hold onto him by his cape. He flashes his peepers, a hundred expressions all in one go; he fires them off in quick succession, his eyebrows talking.

I stare at the photographs on the wall behind him. I don't know what to say; I'm too embarrassed to introduce myself.

To tell the truth I'm dazzled due to his silver mac and glistening goatee to match. He stands there gleaming like my father, a cutie on each arm . . . from Thailand, their belly buttons showing.

To tell the truth, this Sex Pope of their's welcomes me with open arms. He smiles at me and motions for me to get down on my knees so's he can bless me. He parts his cloak and makes as if to put his cock in my mouth. I jump up double quick. Only joking!

The others all laugh at me and even I have to pretend that I think it's funny. Then he goes and does a little circuit of the foyer, chasing his cuties in circles, their tits jiggling, goose-flesh, up-turned. He comes to a halt and starts back on his sermon.

'German women? Danish women? Turkish women? *Scheisse*! . . . they don't want to fuck!' He's on that one again. He goes into overdrive. 'He's not a German, he's a Frenchman! He was in the concentration camps and only escaped by the skin of his teeth!' I already know: it takes a Frenchman to really service a woman, to know her most intimate needs and what she really wants, which is apparently The Sex Pope.

I nod slightly and study my fingers. To try not to appear too rude . . . actually, this Sex Pope makes me feel a little sad, because somehow, no matter what, he can never really be a father to me. And even if I could stand silently before him and keep myself from crying, he would never take me into his arms and embrace me like a true son, or accept me unconditionally for who I really am.

I put my finger into the old cigarette burn in the back of my hand. There's this thick crusty scab and, if I press it, pus spurts out from round the sides.

A young writer runs from one adopted family to the next adopted family, seeking acceptance from all manner of thieves and rascals, hoping beyond all hope to find some perfect reflection in the mirror of some deplorable old Fagin, and thereby to find a little peace in the world for his troubled heart. But all along it is in the vicious spite of his peers that he is most likely to find himself.

And so I hate my new friends and they in turn despise me, and I blame them for having the audacity to live and to breathe, when of course it should be me alone who is put out to stud, like a heavy-bollocked male and told to mate with all the young girls. Of course, what I really hate about my friends is the same as that which I most loathe within myself – which is too painful for me to ever understand and must therefore never be disclosed.

The band shuffle off and start bringing in their instruments. 'Reload the gear! Unload the gear!' That's some word:

'unload the gear!' I've heard that one a million times: 'Load the gear! Unload the gear!' I know all about it. Also I know that it's a phrase and not a word, but that's what it's like being William Loveday. I spit on my palms. 'Unload the gear!' That encompasses everything, stairs, the fire-escape, ten flights, and the whole lot of them drunk. No flunkies, they do it all by themselves. Slaves to the amplifier and valets to the PA. Valves, not transistors! Valves weigh something, they embody a sound. You wouldn't know anything about it. They know what the mugs want – pain, and to pay for it through their ears!

I'm trying to tell you that those fellows were misplaced; they came from a different era. Pre-computer! Pre-transistor! They actually played and performed, old-time style . . . theatre! They're not a recording, they live and they die by their sound. No monitors. No off-stage mixing. Just them in the flesh, hiding behind their little music stands . . . They stand by their noise.

They pick up the horse and cart and it trundles along to the entrance. I put my feet up and have a cigarette.

I do as I'm told and carry in the box with my triangle in it. I place it up on stage. A Sunday night re-opening of Hamburg's famous Star Club, a one-off gala performance.

I tune and de-tune my triangle. A naked Thai girl brings a tray of drinks. The band teetering over the precipice, one false move and it will all be over, a landslide into hell, between the devil's tits – *Ker-boom!* into the orchestra pit.

The ship's crew huddles in the corner like a bush, quivering in the dark, where all the candles and vibrators collect. You have to watch where you tread, one half's completely rotten and the other half's being raffled off.

The auctioneer bangs down his hammers and the whole stage shimmies like a belly-dancer. He shouts and hollers over the din, waving a black cloud of old cloth above his head. Great billows of dust and grit . . . a two-thousand-year-old shroud, one hundred per cent original! He pulls a pair of secateurs from his waistcoat pocket and hacks off great swathes of material, completely moth-eaten; he hands us a shred each.

The dwarf wags his head like a mangy little dog, snatches up the whole lot and stuffs it into his bass drum, and that's the last we'll ever see of it, I shouldn't wonder. A piece of history lost for good. He folds it into his drum case.

'I'm going to make it into ties,' he yodels, and rattles his snare like a machine gun. The show must go on.

I put a brave face on and grin through the danger. I smile up at the sweethearts in the little brothel upstairs, hanging over the balcony – their dusky teats hanging down, inviting you to take a suck; and us down here in the flea-pit, scratching ourselves like monkeys.

The night drags on. I decide I've had enough and take a little jig down the catwalk, a kind of fuck-ramp that slopes off into the audience – a drawbridge over the precipice. I climb on, still clasping my rusty triangle, and my feet slip from under me. I lose my footing and slither down into the audience. It's been greased, that's my honest opinion; the secretions of a thousand nights, fish oil and Vaseline, totally treacherous.

I can't get a grip; the sole of my shoe is coming off, and it flaps like a kipper; I look back up onto the stage and try to figure out a way of getting back to the orchestra when suddenly I'm surrounded. They grind at me: two hefty frauleins. I'm caught between them, mother and daughter. That explains everything. They jig up and down and smile at me horribly; I want to rejoin my friends on the stage, but it's too late. A breast clangs into my triangle.

The old bag's come to re-live her past. She wants to know where Karl Valentin's dressing room is. A tit flops out and smacks me right in the mush. I have to concentrate, just to remember my patterns. Then she turns, bends over, and gyrates her anus at me. That knocks my tuning completely out. I have to bite my lip just to remember my patterns. I'm trapped between the relic of yesteryear and the precipice. Helpless, really. The old frau smooches right up to me and tassles my hair. She pinches my cheek and plants a smacker on my forehead. Can't she see that I'm trying to concentrate?

She grabs me by the scruff of the neck and clambers up onto the stage, dragging me and her kleine fraulein behind her. We get caught up in her slip stream. I get sucked in right behind her.

I make it back to the group and smile timidly in recognition. The old frau shakes herself all over, the stage creaks and slants off. We're capsizing. I cling onto my music stand through the avalanche. The dust of one hundred years ... termites ... the buckling of the boards ... an enormous breast sways before me ... mesmerising, like a balcony ... then I feel the earthquake; the tremors of what's to come, a distant rumbling.

The old frau drags me round the stage like a kitten, then the hurricane breaks loose ... the tinkling of glass ... a bottle drops, a little explosion, a face full of froth, and another. The boards shudder, a rush of cold air goes up my trouser leg and the precipice opens between my feet. I hold onto my little glass of gut-rot and a twenty-inch golden vibrator rolls across the stage and drops – *plop!* – into the abyss. A terrible silence ringing in my ears, the sound of people wondering. I look to the others; a whole minute clocks ... then the sound of muffled cries and scrabbling from the dungeon below. We let out our breath ... lost voices ... eerie ... inexplicable. I hesitate and miss a few chords ... they went straight through; it was nobody's fault, just high spirits. A trail of whiskies – trebles, quadruples. The audience peeps over the edge, smiling through the dust. They try to understand but they're stupid.

Actually the lights get in my eyes. I give up, I've had enough. It's the Thai girls' fault. They distracted me. They've got their little titties out; sticky-out and pointy, the type that give you a hard-on right away. They bring more trays of booze. Glasses, half pints full to the brim. I'm not joking.

I need a break, that's plain as day. The orchestra is running out of ditties, including repeats. I trip over, quite unintentionally, but nobody offers to help me up. I have to pick myself from the floor, then stand and fall over again.

'Somebody,' I shout, 'is rocking the ship!'

I don't really want to upset my new friends but then I go and play the wrong notes on purpose, just to spite myself and for the joy of hearing them berate me.

The one with the side-whiskers screams in my face. The show's over, everything grinds to a halt. The dust settling. I lay down my little triangle as if it was a baby.

'I'll be back in a minute. I'll just take five and I'll be right back. I just want to take a look upstairs, that's all. For the sake of posterity.'

Actually, I can't play another note. I drop my beater; it dances across the boards and jumps down a knot hole and into the dungeon below. I listen out for it but it's gone, lost for good. I make out a face behind the curtain and shrug my shoulders. There's a little plink as it hits the water below and that's it, into the swamp, the stirrings below. I climb down off the stage and merge with the red velvet. Enough is enough, so to speak.

Somebody in a black hat wants to take my photograph, but for once I'm not in the least bit interested; my ego's lost in fascination. I stumble after the dusky buttocks. Up the stairway to the old balcony . . . I follow them right the way to the end. Little shag holes . . . partitioned off . . . funky, laced with that special perfume: acrid. Like some strange, exotic incense, battling to smother the stench of piss and cum.

It makes your teeth itch, that aroma . . . and the closeness of the walls, shuffling through those corridors, feeling your way through the red velvet. You have to mind where you put your fingers in that dump . . . a drinks cabinet . . . the bar . . . I find the corner table and park my arse . . .

I congratulate myself and slap my own back. Where's my drink? Our Sex Pope is nowhere to be seen. A tiny Thai girl bows before me and says hello with her breasts. I have to sit on my hands and look into my empty drink. Then the rest of the orchestra rolls in.

The cuties jump up and swarm round the dwarf like eager little wasps. In their pathetic opinion he's the cutest. He clambers up onto the sofa and sits there cheesy as a cat. His feet can't even touch the ground, and then his huge head. But they're all over him, tasseling his curls and feeding him milk. It's absolutely true – he meows and purrs just like a kitten.

I can't hide my disgust. I honestly feel embarrassed for him and have to look away. I look up and there's a pack of mongrel dogs in the foyer, actually masturbating onto the floor. One of them, a dark and distant relation of a Great Dane, sniffs one girl's arse and actually gets a pat on the head and fed a biscuit!

The pimps brandish their gold teeth at us and fondle themselves in their pockets. It seems that we've jumped the queue, over-stepped the mark and cornered the whole market, so to speak. Apparently we're keeping the paying clientele waiting.

The judge and the Chief of Police? They stare bug-eyed at our table, their little night lights glowing like pin-pricks in the night. For once the fat cats are kept waiting. They inflate themselves, twiddling their podgy fingers and stroking at their zippers. Between them they pull some pretty sour faces, but the Dwarf's oblivious, he loves the world . . . a happy little party. Nobody's spoiling his fun . . . a strange justice . . .

He coughs and walks his thick fingers down the back of the shiny black girl, who turns and shows her gappy teeth. He coos in her ear, romantic as a lovebird. And over in his corner the dark little pimp lifts his glass, grins his sharp gnashers, and shows his glinting blade under the table. It's no joke – these cuties are a hundred marks a throw. He stares over at me, looking me up and down; from my busted shoes to my ghostly face. He chews at his lips, flecked with foam. I try to smile and show him my empty palms. I try reason: it's not as if I'm my brother's keeper. Is it my fault that the dwarf's young and frisky? That he's got more spunk in him than all these old farts put together?

The dwarf tries to nibble his sweetheart's ear, but she's gone all jumpy. 'You saw us playing for free, now it's our turn. How about it, baby?' The dwarf smooches up to her elbow. That word 'baby' sticks in his throat like a ball of dough. His tongue goes all thick but he says it anyway.

'How about it, baby?' He chokes it out through the dust and takes a nip on his whisky bottle. Then the black girl shakes her head, stands and sways backwards. The dwarf jumps down from his perch and comes after her.

'No,' she says.

The dwarf jumps at her waist and pushes the table over.

'Look at them, they're fucking whores, the fucking lot of them!' He pulls at his beard. 'Look, she's got her fucking tits out – put them away!' He shouts orders, puckering up his little gob into a cat's arse. He sucks on his little cigarette and explodes his head in a puff of smoke. 'They're fucking disgusting, look at them!' He turns and argues with himself in the mirror and tries to steal his own drink from his hand.

The black girl looks me up and down as if I'm not really a man at all. She smiles knowingly. I try to tell her about myself, about my poetry and painting, about my heart and my feelings but I may as well go and cut my throat; she's not in the least bit interested. Then her pimp minces over, palming back his hair. He narrows his eyes like a shark. No touching the merchandise until he sees the colour of our money. And no more free drinks. So we're a personal friend of The Sex Pope? Big deal, we can go and frig ourselves at his expense!

'Hey, that's not very friendly!' I stand up to explain, to make sure he knows just who he's talking to and he pushes me in the chest. Then his mates all come bundling over looking for a punch up. They jostle me up against the wall and a bottle almost gets spilt. I try to explain to them politely but it's pointless and then everybody starts shouting at me in a very fast and loud language that I don't understand.

The dwarf hits his head against the mirror and tells them that they're all fucking sluts and ponces and they should all fuck off! The bassoonist has his hand under the table and one of the girls is smiling.

I put my glass down calmly and gently and try to give the

littlest pimp a handshake. I want to pick him up like a toy and see if he squeaks. I introduce myself to him and tell him the names of all my new friends. I introduce him to my black girlfriend and even offer him my seat, but apparently he's got the manners of a pig. He doesn't want to dance, his mother isn't a whore and he wants me out of 'his fucking club' pronto!

The whole gang of them surround us, pushing and shoving me; ushering me out in a most undignified and unfriendly manner. And the rest of their so-called guests applaud them, which is rude and real charming of them, no manners whatsoever. I'm escorted to the door, humiliated in front of their guests and in two shakes I'm out on my arse!

'Excuse me, but that is not very friendly, *Mein Host*!'

The dwarf hangs back, mobbed at the doorway. One girl, the one they call little Tina, hands him a folded note. She wants him to meet her after work. She pinches his wizened cheek and he grins gratefully up at her. The bouncer looms over her shoulder . . . whispered words . . . hurried.

She holds the dwarf by his collar. She finishes at four thirty, he's to wait for her across the street . . . under the awning . . . out of sight, out of mind . . . under the bucking bronco . . . wait for her signal. The dwarf reminds her of her boyfriend back in Thailand, the exact same eyes . . . ah, sweet! Me? I crouch in the rain looking hopefully to the wall of blank faces, right up until the bouncer lets the door go smack in my face.

A small piece of paper floats to the ground: a free ticket to the sex show, signed by The Sex Pope. I pocket it and retreat to the park.

This is the story of my dream. If I want to, I tell myself, I can hang myself. But what if I had been a soldier in the Great War? Which, judging by my sensitive nature, I most probably was. Then, it's more than likely that I would be a Lance Corporal in the Royal West Kent Regiment and my name would be Jack, or Simon, or some other such name, and that I would have to grow a moustache.

And if I was this fellow Jack or Simon, then it's quite probable that his ghost still lives within me until this day, which is a terrifying thought.

I would most probably be in charge of some Lewis gun section and the chances are that I would be sent by my commanding officer to some forward position in the front line, accompanied by two of my old muckers from my school days – someone like Marshland or Ian Woollcut, for instance.

It would be daytime in early spring and the mounds of red earth from the freshly dug trenches would be piled high on the brand new parapets.

Occasionally rifle fire would whine over our heads, followed by the scream of a heavy shell coming over and a great spurt of mud would vomit up into the clear blue sky as artillery boomed in the distance.

After Stand two, I would no doubt peer through a chink in the parapet and see the gradual advance of a little grey line of men coming through the spoiled corn. I would feel the cold metal of the Lewis gun in my hand; then, lifting its weight, scream at the top of my lungs and fling it to the bottom of the ditch. Next, I turn and run screaming down the line of trenches, towards our own back line, my breath coming in snatched grunts. My comrades would be clawing at my arms, imploring me to stop and come back but I would just keep on running, dragging them in my wake; my eyes staring like a madman repeating over and over: 'Never! Never! Never!' on my inward breath and I would hug my words towards my heart and my boots would sound loudly on the newly-laid duck boards as I charge past the lifted and startled faces of my countrymen.

Next, a broad-shouldered sergeant would have to stand roughly forth, block my path and smash me in the face with his great hairy fist and I would spin bleeding and blubbering to the bottom of the trench.

Later that night I might wake cold and shivering, a captive in the crypt of some Belgian chapel and just lie there forever, waiting for the dawn. After an impossible age it would finally break and shine its new light on me. A vicar and two grim-faced guards would no doubt come, the gaoler jangling his keys at me and I would be led from that dark place out into the blinding sunlight where I would momentarily see the terrified faces of my two companions before a coarse sack is pulled roughly over my head and I feel my hands being bound tightly behind my back.

Then, next to a crumbling wall in those shell-torn cloisters, they would most likely force us to our knees and execute all three of us.

My last feeling of this world would be of the roughness of the sacking tied at my neck; its harsh smell would assault my sensitive nostrils and little dots of light dance before my eyes. Then suddenly hot needles would smash into my chest and I would be flung down rudely to one side.

My spirit would most probably have risen out of me by this time and I would be able to look down on myself and see the scared white faces of my executioners, their eyes painful behind the thin veil of acrid smoke that rises from their rifles.

I can also see the immature moustache twitch slightly on the silly little lip of the sandy-haired officer, who walks over and fires a single shot from his revolver into my poor head.

Next, I watch my feet kick and twitch as I die, and a strange feeling rises from the back of my skull as my heels lift from the ground and I ascend backwards up into the heavens. Below me I see the scene of my death, my corpse lying prostrate between the empty bodies of my two friends in the dew-heavy grass. And up over the wall the surrounding panorama of countryside. The little lanes; a troop of merry soldiers headed for the front. Some horses innocently pulling munitions, apparently unaware of their complicity and probably a great feeling of sadness would pervade in my heart and I would cry for my lost youth – to die so young and to have never known love.

And I wouldn't be able to help but be angry with my

wretched father for sending me away to that spiteful war, and I would long for the beautiful countryside of north Kent.

And at home, in some village like West Malling, there would be my sweetheart who I had shared longing glances with during the hay-making last summer, and she would sob uncontrollably for me, that I was gone and that we would never know the secrets of each other's young bodies.

A city is a lovely place to trudge in the rain. A lost soldier in a foreign town. The harsh chisel faces of their blond women rebuff a young fellow at every turn.

When I awoke this morning, there was a little crust of frost covering my trembling body. I had walked half the night through these German streets and found nothing but the cold smiles of an arrogant and indifferent nation. No matter how miserably I coughed and tried to spit blood, nothing came up.

Whenever an elegant-looking lady approached me, I cunningly stooped, held onto my stomach and moaned slightly, but not one of them stopped to console me, or feed me, or invite me back to their luxurious bedrooms. No, not one of them gave me so much as one single miserly glance as they passed me by, my hungry eyes being dragged up the street after them.

It seems that the race of women has no time for the sufferings of their most accursed enemy: man. And any gentleness that rests in my heart only compounds their loathing for me, hating me all the more for not being a worthy opponent on the battleground of sex. So, like any poor foot soldier in need of shelter and a bed, I am as loathed by my own generals as I am by those of the enemy.

I step on, my busted shoe flapping furiously, echoing on the harsh streets, until I stumble down here to the fish market to sleep on their charming beach. The hard cobbles rise up like babies' heads and grind into my tender spine.

Round about dawn I notice a deep malignant ache growing steadily within my left hip, and smile grimly to myself. It is good to know that my mother's and father's neglect is finally going to damage my very essence. Whilst they are sunning themselves on the beaches of paradise their precious son is contracting arthritis and double pneumonia, sleeping on what can best be described as jagged icy rocks.

I lie here in reverie, trying to stem my chattering teeth. At this precise moment my parents will be strolling side by side on their South Sea Island. My mother will of course be hanging back slightly, wearing her sunglasses, her head tilted shamefully away from the faces of passing strangers, hiding the black eye that my father had dished out to her over the breakfast table.

It is true to say that when I was young I dressed in my mother's clothes, walked the streets exposing myself to passing traffic and had sex with the family dog. But that doesn't necessarily make me a dog lover, or mean that I should forever be punished for the sins of my father. After all, it is my father who left me when I was seven, not I who left him!

Quickly I jump up; a young writer could get rheumatism lying about on these streets in mid winter. I look fearfully at the shiny black cobbles and wonder if the cold and damp really has penetrated me to the extent that I shall suffer from rheumatism.

I give myself permission to sit on a nearby bench and try to rub some life back into my aching limbs. A bell chimes seven o'clock and a little bird starts up singing in the darkness. I get up and walk to the bushes, listening out for his song. I try to spot him but it's still very dark and the streetlight is broken.

I decide that rather than becoming rich by suffering, my fortunes lie in the city. So I hobble off in that direction, hoping to be rescued by a rich countess.

Perhaps if I just stay hunched up on the ground long enough, then maybe her horse-drawn carriage will pass by in the cold dawn and I will be recognised as the true, noble poet that I am, and thence be driven off to her wonderful palace in the countryside; where I will no doubt meet and fall in love with her beautiful, sexual daughter.

I realise that this is a ridiculous notion, probably brought on by the icy winds that have constantly blown at my exposed neck throughout the dreadful night. But no matter how strongly I resist the temptation I can't help believing that I have a crisp, rosy-red apple in my pocket which I shall feed the countess's lead horse.

Good news – today I have found somewhere else to live. It is in a charming frozen park. There is a derelict car in a little grotto amongst the trees and every morning a man comes on his bicycle to feed the stray cats.

He carries one of them, a small white kitten, in the wicker basket that hangs from his handlebars. In one motion he drives past, snatches up the kitten – quite violently – and plunks it down in his basket. Apparently, the cat quite enjoys the sensation, as it puts up no resistance and is quite happy to ride around the park in this manner.

On my walk about town today I discovered a teashop where down-and-outs can get a cup of char. I adjust my milk churn hat and look to my broken shoe. The teahouse is full. I hold out my white, trembling hands to them all, but not one of them accepts my kind gesture or pours me a hot drink and slowly I am pushed out onto the street. I lose my grip on the doorframe, my elbow slips and I have to wave goodbye as they fling me onto the cold cobblestones.

Once again I crouch in the rain, looking hopefully up at the wall of blank faces; right up until that door too is slammed shut in my face.

I pick myself from the floor, put my sailor's cap back on my head, cross the road that they call the Reeperbahn, and head back towards the docks. That's where I see them: a great horde of rude women sat naked behind the plate glass windows.

One, with a painted face, gurns through glass at me. Then all of her friends start banging on their windows with their fists. There is a terrible pounding and their jewellery rattles at me.

A large, sexual black woman turns and points her buttocks in my direction, then sticks her fingers into her mouth and sucks on them whilst looking right at me. She has a friend in there with her who lifts her breasts out of her vast golden bra and offers them up to me like a pair of disintegrating pancakes and I have to hunt around in my pockets, looking for something I have forgotten.

There are many men crowding the pavement outside and they look at me aggressively, before turning back to the windows and jeering with their loud voices.

It seems that the people of the German nation have all decided to let me know that I am not even welcome upon their shores. The faces all look at me threateningly and shove me to the back of the crowd until my feet are once again stood in the gutter. I try to stand on my tiptoes and peer over their heads but they hunch their backs and raise their shoulders to purposely block my view. Their disapproval hangs in the air like vapour. Apparently I have been walking along with my head on backwards, my bellbottoms flapping like flags at my knees, and a badge of the hangman on my forehead. This is the reason they mock me.

I stare at my blue-veined hands. I press one of the veins with my finger. It is important that nobody finds out how sensitive I am. I let myself slump against a lamppost and dribble down my sleeve.

The cold wind finds its way into my mouth and hurts my teeth. Across the street is an all-night cafe. Whenever the door opens great billows of smoke and steam rise up into the night. I imagine eating something but my hunger has somehow gone out and I can no longer feel anything in my poor stomach.

If I was the orchestra's banker, which in certain ways I am, I would certainly keep all of my money safely stashed in my front trouser pocket – which is risky and swashbuckling.

I have walked round in a vast circle and find myself back outside the sex club. There is a large crowd gathered. The dwarf is there waiting with two of the ship's crew but the others haven't shown yet. They don't say hello to me so I go in alone.

I hand in my ticket and am re-greeted by his holiness. The Sex Pope stands there like a wizard, dressed in the finest of Japanese silks. I know the score by now: he blesses me and I have to bow. He introduces his Thai girls again and tries to tell me how smart he is and then the dwarf comes in, followed by the rest of the crew.

The Sex Pope smiles around the room and rubs his hands together. He twirls the ends of his moustache and laughs right in my face. Drinks all round! The bottle tips. He wants to ensure that everybody's comfortable, that there's nothing more that we desire. His hands fly like birds ... and a little faded tattoo on his wrist ... his number from the concentration camps ...

He fills everybody's glasses to overflowing and then shows everyone to their seats, personally you understand. He plays everything for effect. Hooded eyes, theatrical. He bows, then departs ... he's got to go; he says his good-byes. He'd like to stay but there's his choreography. His masterpiece!

He kisses his fingertips, rubs himself and exits. He's needed elsewhere. He doesn't need to explain himself to me. I watch him merge into the smoke.

Everything in that place is draped in the same heavy velvet: blood-red, hanging down in great festoons. Curtains and drapes, layer upon layer, miles of the stuff, intricate folds ... blurred. All in red ... absolutely. Even the wallpaper. Flock, maroon spirals, paisley. The seats are real soft to the touch, too.

A great chandelier swings to and fro from the intricate ceiling. I tell myself that all the wood work is decorated with little flying cherubs flecked with real gold but then refuse to check whether or not it's true. I stare at the old chipped plaster of paris that hangs from the corners of the stage and a terrible anger burns up inside of me. Whole noses of exquisite cherubim have been smashed off and ground down into the stinking, revolting carpet. All the fittings in gold leaf? My foot!

I really have to stop myself from laughing at their pathetic, squalid little theatre.

I look round at the grim faces that surround me and have to resist the urge to get up and walk out. I tell myself that I should bite my armrest. I really am about to leave when an expectant hush descends over the auditorium. The music quietens, the curtains shimmering slightly. The show's about to begin.

A little row of fat faces peep over the balcony up the back, their noses drooping like melted plastic. A thousand cigarettes are burning ... great swirls of smoke ... a man farts – *Phut!* Then, through the fog a small figure appears. The Frog Man emerges, dragging himself along on his terrible little belly, his legs painted luminescent green; a slithering movement by the curtains, and out he hops, hiccupping.

He stands there caught in the spotlight like a startled amphibian who, to the best of its knowledge, had expected to surface in an enchanted pool next to a tinkling fountain and be fed a number of choice slugs from the hand of a naked princess. Of course, no one can be absolutely certain that this is exactly what was running through this Frog Man's mind, but we do know that he next belched and waved his little webbed paw at us. He blinks and gives two more little hiccups to set the tone exactly right.

Messieurs, mesdames, meine damen und herren, Ladies and Gentlemen,' he croaks. 'May we present to you tonight's theme – Sex and the Fall of the Roman Empire. And so, without further ado, live from Pompeii – Death In The Whore House!' Exit the performing frog and bring on the dancing girls, legs splayed and tits throbbing.

An usherette pushes past me and accidentally steps on my foot. She smiles her mask at me then goes down on her knees and sticks her crusty face into the lap of the old scrote sat opposite me. I sink back and pretend not to be looking. His eyes roll back into his fist-sized skull, like a pair of glass marbles that some careless child has dropped onto the pavement, and then looks on excitedly as they roll inexorably towards the gutter.

The beautiful maiden sticks out her coated tongue and starts lapping at his milky old stalk like a kitten lapping at a bowl of sour yoghurt.

The old man wriggles his bony pelvis and jiggles in his seat. I rub my burning eyes, the spectacle filling me with horror and fascination. Soon I will look under my seat but I refuse to lick the carpet.

Right in front of me is the neck of a fat businessman, its furrows and creases jammed into his collar like a piece of cooked spam. A spotlight spins round the room and shines clean through his ears like X-Rays ... half moons in pink ... blinding reflections bouncing right off his shimmering pate.

A screaming fanfare barks out at us and two sirens of the deep appear from out of some calico waves. Each grimacing princess stands framed in an individual balcony of fake gold.

They scan the audience and pout right at us, totally unabashed. Then, on an in-breath, they start their slow, merciless grind, false teeth flashing, their skin glowing hideous hues of orange and russet. Both of them are done out in matching crepe curtains and gold sashes.

The audience lug on their cigarettes and great lungfuls of purple smoke billow up, filling the air with their thick plumes. The sirens croon their songs of the deep. Horny Hilda toys with her anchor and wags her red, bloated tongue at the dwarf. It glistens in the spotlights, as thick as a saveloy.

The dwarf sits there totally mesmerised, sucking on his cigarette till he burns his lips. He wastes no time in telling all and sundry exactly where his affections lie. Hilda stares him right in the eye, head erect, tits magnificent, pointing, accusing ... five-inch heels and calf muscles like cricket balls!

The dwarf wags his head like a sick cobra, following every bump and grind of her plastic hips, right down to her last nylon G-string ... he rubs his peepers till they squeak ... then she turns, twisting and writhing like a wolverine ... one last tug at the satin and out it pops – a small brown fellow, bald as a Chinaman. It juts out just above her cunt, peeping out of the sparse hairs, little drapes of flesh hanging below it. No balls at all; just a little pair of shabby beef curtains.

Hilda shakes her old chap at the audience. She pounds it against her thighs and belly with great resounding slaps – *Thudump! Thudump!* Back and forth and from side to side. She sprays the whole front row – *Thudump! Thudump!* And then she turns and exits, the drawing of a dragon tattooed clean down the centre of her spine – and the red and gold sashes crash together and engulf her ... She disappears, swallowed back into the womb.

The dwarf droops his head like a tortoise. He looks round the room in slow motion, his mouth opening and closing on an imaginary piece of lettuce. He can't get over it ... *Thudump! Thudump!* And the sashes crash together. He's positively crest-fallen. The magic's completely gone out of his evening. Actually, he's not in the least bit abashed; he stamps and whistles louder than anyone.

The audience hardly has time to swallow its spit before the music blares out anew and the next turn, sultry Marlene, hobbles onto the boards bathed in screaming reverb ... echoing ... languid and rouged.

'Lilli Marlene,' she croaks.

We're caught laughing, which is impolite. She comes lickity-split, rushing the audience. She slings down her microphone and jams her fingers into her glue-pot, scooping out great fistfuls of sauce. She smiles and ladles it out, running from row to row smearing the batter under the clientele's noses, filling their moustaches. The audience ducks and dives, the stench rising. I take a deep breath and sit as far back in my seat as it will allow.

I lower my head sarcastically and hook my thumbs into my belt-loops. I lift my feet from the floor in case of crocodiles. Then the sound of her approaching feet ... her mouth twisted, a low gurgling noise coming from somewhere deep in her throat. She receives some stout kicks from sailors. They aim with precision and hold out their lighted cigarettes as a cordon.

She tries to sit on the bassoonist's lap but he accidentally burns her nipple with his clove-flavoured cigarette. Marlene jumps up and snarls at him like a she-wolf. A man in a silver-fox-fur coat stands and gives her a vicious shove and a boot, which in my opinion is unnecessary. He climbs onto the back of his seat and gives it a good dogging. He gnaws at the wood and smiles at me. Marlene sneaks up behind him, jumps onto his back and rubs her poor body into the glistening fur. She wants him to eat her paste for her. She holds onto his ears and slaps a handful into his chops. He bucks and thrashes, screws up his nose and throws her clean over his head. Marlene holds on by her calves, grinding her pelvis into the silver-fox. It rolls like a fur wave then bucks and flings her into the night. She sails through the dark air, then crashes down into the front stalls; her shins ricocheting between the mahogany armrests. She rolls into a bruised heap and lets out a loud grunt.

Actually, I feel sorry for her and want to protect her, but on the other hand she revolts me and I feel she deserves whatever she's got coming to her and a thrill of naughtiness runs clean up my spine. The dwarf does the gentlemanly thing and helps her to her feet.

Marlene crawls to her hands and knees and limps round in little circles, whimpering like a whipped mutt. It's all for effect, she's just fishing for people's sympathies. She sulks and pouts, then turns on us and swears like a fish wife. Actually, she has a large, black mole on her Adam's apple, which I refuse to look at.

Basically, the dwarf goes soft in the head and falls for her, hook, line and sinker. He feels sorry for the poor *kleine liebling*. He flutters his handkerchief at her and wipes at her cracked mug. First one tear, then the next . . . he woos her and rubs her bruised buttocks.

'There, there!' She perches on his tiny lap, sucks on a grollie and manages a brave smile, her bony chest heaving. The Dwarf laps at her singed nipple and she cradles his massive head in her ape-like fists. She puts her finger to his lips and traces a line through his coarse beard and round his funny mouth. She chucks him under the chin then jams her great tongue down the back of his throat. I see it dive, salmon-like, then I have to look away out of politeness. They're getting pretty intimate down there. Kissing and canoodling like that; completely oblivious. It really is enough to make you blush.

The Frog Man coughs irritably. He taps his baton against the music stand and beckons to Marlene with it.

Marlene looks up and reluctantly extracts her tongue. She takes away the dwarf's hands, folds them on his lap and without any further ado flits back onto the stage.

She turns all coy, wriggles her slim hips at the dwarf and blows him a kiss. Great cracks of mascara running down her face like black lava. She flutters her falsies – *Blink! Blink!* Two spiders, and she's gone – back up the fuck-ramp and into the labyrinth beyond. Lost in the drapes, just a glimpse, a fleeting shadow ... *Blink! Blink!* ... She's definitely gone.

She certainly knows how to break a fellow's heart. The dwarf chews at his fingers and implores God. He wants his Marlene back, he must have her! 'Did we see the way she looked at him?' He fidgets around in his seat trying to catch her eye, rubbing his knees together in frustration. There's no doubt that he thinks he's pulled.

He looks around the room and assumes a smug air, fondling his velvety lapels and winking at complete strangers. He becomes unbearable, swaggering and taking bigger and bigger swigs at his scotch. He even lights up his pipe and sits there spitting sparks – a calabash as big as his head.

It really is as if he is some small elf-like creature who, after making friends with some mischievously disguised hobgoblin, is apparently totally unaware that the shiny red apple he has been given is in fact a piece of rotting, poisonous fruit. Then, polishing it on his chest, he sits down on a conveniently placed toadstool and starts munching away on the maggoty old apple, happy that his life should have taken such a lucky turn.

The one with the red side-whiskers takes it upon himself to

break the news ... to tell the dwarf the score, as diplomatically as possible, before he invites the whole theatre to the wedding. He takes his foot out of his mouth and comes straight out with it. Actually, those sailors are very bold in telling the dwarf just what type of a complete and utter idiot he really is. It seems that our vivacious Marlene is none other than Max, an ex-lorry driver. The dwarf stares straight ahead and says nothing. I see his lips quiver and then he brings his hands up and strokes his overly large chin.

The sailors study him as the penny drops. Fat, vicious smiles spreading across their ugly lips.

The dwarf gets the picture. It dawns on him slowly. He swallows and nods, staring off into the shadows, avoiding their eyes. He comes over all sheepish, jumps down and starts rummaging around in the dust. He sticks his toe under the seat in front, looks up and kind of smiles, his lips trembling.

The ringleader leans back and spits. He opens his gob as wide as it will go, stamps his feet and laughs out loud, rubbing his hands together with glee. He does a little jig. He's pleased as punch. That really makes his day – somebody else has been taken! He laughs right in the dwarf's face and his mates join in too.

All the while the dwarf just sits there puffing on his ridiculous pipe, which he can barely hold in his miniature fists. Quite frankly he doesn't believe a word of it. His little fraulein? Such a sweet temperament, such manners, such finesse. And her hands, they were so small and attractive. Nobody really wants to contradict him, but still ... he takes off his jacket, ready for a punch-up. He'll take on any dirty bastard who dares to even suggest such a thing! He knocks over somebody's popcorn, ready to fight the whole auditorium. He puts his fist right up under one sailor's nose. The audience jeers at him.

The sailors have to assure him that, just because Marlene is a man, it doesn't mean that he finds her any less attractive. Moustache or no moustache, she's probably got a lovely personality.

The dwarf narrows his eyes. He looks at them sulkily and tells them all to watch it, or else! At last he climbs back up onto his seat, pulls out his pipe and stuffs it back in his gob. He sucks down a great lungful and coughs. He splutters, examining the bowl.

The stage bows and tips, shimmering like clingfilm. My eyes can't adjust to the glaring lights. I stare through that night and a terrible clamouring fills my ears, a grinding of cogs and gears as they lower a great cloud from out of the rafters, which is quite frightening. It swings to and fro on steel cables . . . a ton of cotton wool, great billows of the stuff, and a little man sat grinning on top, hands on hips, cock flexed. The Mighty Zeus. He smiles his spongy lips at the audience and stares down, transfixed by his own manliness. He comes from out of the darkness wafting down onto the stage below. Pompous, authoritarian and erect, but still one of the lads, so to speak. In short – an impossible effect.

From out of the orchestra pit a great drumroll builds and builds until finally filling the entire building with its reverberations.

It's time for little Tina to be broken in. The Mighty Zeus awaits her, sat astride his fake cloud, his arms folded on his woman-like chest. Little Tina stands there in the wings, her knees knocking, her face drained but defiant.

She peers out into the audience for the dwarf. She looks to him lovingly but not a hint of emotion shows on his face. He is not in the least bit interested. He refuses to acknowledge her.

The audience is torn two ways. On the one hand they feel sorry for her, but on the other they laugh anyway, out of sheer spite. Actually the whole auditorium howls like monkeys, banging on the backs of their seats and spilling their beer over the upholstery, no better than microbes.

Zeus lifts his index finger and beckons. He nods to his maleness, blue-veined, wavering through the cigarette smoke . . . I have to look, even though I tell myself that I will become a homosexual.

Little Tina shakes her head in despair, clenches her tiny fists and stamps her foot. She looks imploringly to the dwarf but he resolutely ignores her.

Tina turns and pleads for one of the other chorus girls to take her place, just for this one show. But one after another they shake their heads in gloomy refusal. Little Tina's got to face the music alone. The lights dazzling her, the poor girl's not up for it. Not tonight. Not with her dwarf sat out there in the front row.

Little Tina hold her hands protectively in front of her, and a derisive jeer goes up as the audience senses her spirit ebbing away. They roar and stamp their feet, swigging at their beers and blowing out clouds of bitter smoke. I catch a glimpse of a figure moving darkly in the wings, his silver cape and goatee glinting in the shadows; it's The Sex Pope, the old fox! He steps boldly up behind her and kicks her square in the arse. Tina staggers forward across the stage, turns, looks into his hooded eyes, lowers her glance and shuffles meekly out onto the boards.

She adjusts her G-string, takes two or three deep breaths, and strides on swinging her buttocks. She plants herself on the end of Zeus's cloud and gives him a glare to knock him dead. But The Mighty Zeus just smiles nonchalantly, lies back on the cotton wool, flexes his swollen member and nods it in her direction. The audience roars its appreciation.

He really lies there like some disgusting hairy old bear, sprawled out on a bed of stinking goose feathers. And even though I pretend to examine myself and understand what it is that I find so repulsive in this heathen man, really I am just excited by his maleness and am dreaming of the day that it will be me who stands naked upon that stage with the maidens of the world gathered to my loins, suckling my God-like phallus whilst I spray my seed into their open mouths and gratefully upturned faces.

And so I goad myself for secretly grinning at little Tina's fate, forcing myself to look on, to put my tongue in the blood and

guts and taste it streaming from my lips. And I turn and laugh up my sleeve at my discomfort and the discomfort of my fellows; and I tell myself that one day soon I will have to pay for this blasphemy. Which is silly and exciting but probably true.

Little Tina accepts her fate, but she gives Mighty Zeus some pretty vicious looks as he noses it in – a hate-filled expression. The thunder rolls, a flash of neon, four slave girls kneel to the pillars of Aphrodite, no hands! Not even a knee trembles.

I have to take a pee, which is not allowed – ambushes in the dark and the fear of usherettes. I have to pretend that I don't want sex, and in many ways I don't.

By an imperceptible sign the harem disengage themselves and rise from their knees. Marlene reappears. She comes staggering out across the stage, her mask re-fixed. Hungry-eyed, lips burning. She has a moment to gather herself then, taking her cue, slithers down the fuck-ramp and into the audience below. She takes her pick of the businessmen.

The dwarf nods his jowls in anticipation, his neck purpling up, garrotted by his neckerchief. Marlene opens her box in front of him. His tongue lapping at the disgusting lips, his hands trembling as they fumble with her bird's nest.

The dwarf raises his head and leers at me across the back of his seat, grease dripping from his beard and chin, his whole shirt front smeared with sauce. He smiles and carries on filling his boots. The spotlight burns holes clean through both his ears, his skull bone glinting like the sea. The spam starts bubbling but he munches on regardless. The audience grows hushed, appalled by his greed.

Marlene drapes her leg over his shoulder and holds him in a death grip, sucking him in deeper and deeper, grinding her pelvis until you can hear the bones crack. His ears turn from red to purple to black, his hands fluttering through the fog . . . muffled . . . his head sagging. Marlene holds the coot by his ears and pulls him in again. Riding his face, gyrating her synthetic clit into his slobbering gob.

Marlene loosens her grip and he rolls onto his back, a thoughtful expression spreading across his lips . . . then he gags and jumps up retching . . . he slaps at the back of his neck, his face swelling up like a blackberry . . . he goes down on his hands and knees and 'Eeores' like a donkey. Something's jammed in his throat, that much is obvious.

He waves to the ceiling then turns and bows to the left and to the right, his arms jerking through the smoke filled air, his hands massaging at his blocked windpipe. Then with a great heave he yacks up a piece of old rubber. It slithers across the carpet and comes to rest between Marlene's feet. Whereupon our intrepid traveller stands, brushes himself down and, picking the fungus from between his teeth, blushes slightly and sits down.

Old Zeus reappears from out of the wings, marches purposefully down the fuck-ramp and presents himself before the dwarf. He slaps it to attention and it waves, quivering, under the dwarf's nose.

A hush descends over the auditorium as he slaps the dwarf's face with it. We hear each swish of the blade, tempting for some but not for our gourmet, who looks mournfully around the room, blinded by the spotlights, bald and dejected.

The sailors egg him on, screeching in their seats and banging their glasses so hard on the tables that they make the ashtrays jump. Our dwarf wipes his tongue on his cuff and staggers. Zeus makes another grab for him, but the dwarf ducks and sidesteps him, hiccupping all the way. The trouble is that he's lost his appetite. He's got fluff all over his tongue.

Marlene slams him up against the edge of the stage, but again the dwarf wriggles free, dashing between her legs. The audience applauds him, whistling and stamping their feet, they shout until they're hoarse. The dwarf smiles and bows, he apologises, hiding his face in his handkerchief. Then he makes a break for it, scrambling over the seats and disappearing into the velvety drapes, into the funk-laced alcoves beyond. We hear his breath rasping in the shadows, giant gulps . . . a bellows . . . wheezing . . . only drowned out by Zeus's great guffaws of laughter.

The Reeperbahn, all those lights revolving, like a fairground, really, but cars instead of gee-gees. I was drunk, day-dreaming . . . dawdling . . .

'Don't dawdle,' my mother used to say to me. 'You're dawdling, don't dawdle!'

I was looking for butterflies, the little chalk-blue, over the fields on the way to school. That's right, fields, not housing estates, fields! With spider webs . . . 'gossamer webs', that's what my mother called them . . . and the little chalk-blue . . . 'Don't dawdle!'

Hmmm, and the *polizei* drives straight at me, puts his foot down on purpose . . . *Veroomski!* I had to jump . . . *Whoops!* up onto the pavement. He could have hit me driving like that, no doubts about that . . . *Veroomski!* . . . If I hadn't had my wits about me.

He winds his window down, and tells me what for; he jumps in arse first.

'*Ich bin eine Inglander,*' I tell him sarcastically, looking from beneath my beautiful sailor's cap.

That takes the biscuit! He bites on his toothpick and spits blood. He stares down at the juice and then back up to me. He gives me a real look of disgust.

He can't believe his misfortune: for him, an officer of the law, to have to talk to such a man? I'm the lowest of the low, a crawling insect not even worth treading on. He jams his jalopy into gear and skids off someplace else.

'An English dumbkopf? The sole falling off his shoe? He's not even worth arresting!'

Veroomski! Out of sight, out of mind . . . *Veroomski!* Off someplace else, the other end of town, the docks more than likely.

And then the Christmas lights come on. I walk on, enchanted. I follow my nose . . . The tide. There's this hole in the wall, I walk in there and then it opens out into some kind of shell grotto. Some kind of pothole . . . more like a crack in the wall . . .

The comings and goings of humanity, coughing, hunched . . . I lose myself in that sea . . . you have to keep moving . . . the current, I'm sucked in, I'm absorbed . . . pushing and jostling in the darkness of the tunnel. Sour breath, a hacking noise, a burp of beer . . . I hold my head above the stench, then I'm puked out at the other end into a courtyard, like a school playground. Blinking through these constant red lights, like everything's in a cheap home movie. I rub my eyes and blink through the red fuzz, a mush . . . slow-motion, like velvet, red . . . I blink, I wait for my eyes to adjust.

The rain's in here as well, pouring down the walls, across the yard and into this big piss trough in the middle. Terrible squalls, a great iron grid in the centre, the sound of a waterfall cascading into the blackness. And the girls all huddled round these wind shelters, like a bus stop in the rain. Displaying their wares: arsehole and breast – a regular meat market – eyes zonked, chewing on their lips. Hawkish. And up over there, some lighted windows, splodges of neon showing through the drizzle.

'You vont fuch? Vee can fuch. Looks, touches, zee everythings – fifty marks, ja?'

The crowd swallows me up whole, one gulp and I'm gone. Swept from one end of the courtyard to the next.

Where's my fraulein? I walk on, my sole flapping, my socks actually wet through.

The cuties come at me from out of the haze . . . red . . . fuzzy . . . indistinct . . . out of the crowd . . . on shiny red shoes . . . she comes swaying her arse . . . little red velvet shorts . . . she's homed in on me in particular, spotted my unholy mug. I'm really touched, it must be a sign.

'You vont fuch? Fifty marks harf howre.'

I drag my gaze from her silly sling-back shoes, her calves taut . . . and stare into her beautiful eyes, transfixed . . . the make-up a fluorescent film over the grime.

You will be mine tonight, Kursty . . . for I am a man, with a man's desires and passions, and a young writer shouldn't have to spend his nights forever alone.

'I am William Loveday,' I tell her. '*Ich spiele in eine beat gruppa.*' I mime playing the triangle and she stares blankly back at me.

'Who?'

'In die Golden Handshoe. The other night. You remember, the dwarf.' I yell at her with my bloodshot eyes.

'You remember me. I've come to take you away from all of this!' I gesture towards the damp bricks and the hideous neon lights and she looks unrecognisingly into my hot, bloodshot eyes . . . my sweet eyes, my deceitful, filthy, stinking eyes . . . my eyes shaped like little fishy's. And if I could I would snatch them out, throw them to the pavement and stamp on them . . . I appall myself, shouting at a young lady like that, banging my fists without first having the courtesy to ask her name.

'I am sorry. What's your name?' My voice sounds strange to me, somehow distant and far off, as if strangled from another man's throat. And I imagine myself to be from the pit, to not be human at all, but rather some mud-caked zombie, croaking out strange, incoherent sounds. All in the wrong order . . . high pitched . . . trying to impress her . . . I don't like my voice . . . And my hair too . . . I can't get it to go right.

She narrows her eyes, holds me with her cold, hard stare, then she leads me away . . . The click-clack of her heels . . . I follow her arse through the playground, the weight of each cheek on its own spring. She turns and grimaces over her shoulder, encouraging me.

I follow her down the slope, into the big dip . . . over the iron grid that makes a sound . . . and the water below, black, oily . . . *Clang! Clang! Clang!* I have to stop and drop a coin in for luck, ten pfennigs . . . out of my hip pocket. The seconds tick by. I'm about to leave and walk on when I hear it hit the bottom. *Plink!* . . . It echoes back up to me. That's the Elbe down there, we're walking on a marsh; the whole fucking city's perched over a swamp! The dead of ages down there drinking mud.

My little fraulein hollers at me to hurry up . . . 'Don't dawdle!' I look up and race on, I catch up with her and smile, because I want to be liked and be known for my bravery.

She stands there by the doorway, hands on her hips, clattering her painted nails at me.

I drop my coin and hurry on through the crowds, the atmosphere of the impending fuck. Dreams that must end in a little squirt on the floor and a sour goodbye. It's only money, my sweet Kursty! No love. My heart frozen.

She buzzes the door and I hurry on. I just catch her. She folds her arms and waits for me. She yawns and looks meaningfully at her watch. I peep in the doorway at the little gang of pimps, sat playing cards around a knackered old table. One of them looks up at me and she shouts something to him in Turkish.

His face is small and mean. I bow deeply and he puffs out

the last of his ciggie and punches the automatic latch. My lady friend pushes the door and I follow her in under the neon sign . . . right the way down to the end, past all the other numbers, right to the very end . . . room number 133.

'My name is William, William Loveday.'

She folds her arms across her hard breasts and looks at me with her hard flint-like eyes which I love. 'What's yours?' I ask.

She looks slantwise up at the ceiling and lets out a heavy sigh, 'Janet,' she speaks. I try not to stare at her breasts.

'I need to go for a piss, Janet.'

The light in the bog closes my eyes . . . it burns . . . I see stars, a galaxy of dots. I froth up the water, drop my cigarette in and hose him round the pan . . . a harsh yellow jet . . . the smell of myself comes up to me and rests my troubled mind. I shake off the drips and dab at the end of it with a piece of toilet tissue, examining it carefully, checking for blood.

'You tidy dis fings away now!' She points at my trousers. 'You tidy dis fings away now, vee ave tventy minuten only!'

I look at her and light up another cigarette. I fiddle with the box of matches sulkily and take my time. Actually, I drop the whole box on the floor on purpose, hoping to make her angry with me.

She stares at me accusingly and then starts to laugh in an artificial way. She points to my feet, holds her sides and humiliates me on account of the tape holding my shoe together. I refuse to look down and give her the satisfaction of knowing that I know what she's laughing at. I cross my feet and stand on the offending shoe and stare past her. Letting her know, in no uncertain terms, that I am an experienced young writer and have no time for such idiotic things as feet. Actually, I sit down and hide my feet under the bed.

'I lost my sole . . . an accident. . .' I trail off.

I stare at my cigarette and hate it. I couldn't care less and flick the ash on her sad, stupid little carpet.

She fixes me again with her cold flinty eyes and I want her to kiss me and implore me to love her, and then, just as she opens to me, I will turn away and deny her. For she has trifled with a man this time. To teach her some respect. Just to spite her.

'You buy me drink now! You tidy dis fings avay and buy me drink, ja?' She looks down at my raggedy bellbottoms.

'I'll take them off in a minute.'

Janet grimaces, lets out another deep sigh. Apparently I'm boring her.

'You buy drinks now! Ten marks! You have vone tventy marks!'

'I don't vant vone,' I mimic her.

She screws up her mouth like a spoilt little girl, until it isn't the least bit pretty any more, and I realise that I am older than this pathetic little girl-child. I am a man, not a little boy, and she must therefore bend to my will.

'You pay moneys now! Thirty minutes, fifty marks!'

I stretch out my leg, put my hand in my pocket and fiddle with my precious notes. I am in charge of this moment. I peel them off slowly, one by one. I see myself in the mirror and check my hat. I know how to wear a hat and I wear it just right. I admire myself in a sickening sort of way. I pull the notes out of my back pocket and peek at them coyly. Janet snatches the notes from my hand, counts out fifty marks on the bed and then folds them away into her red plastic purse. She hands me back the loose change.

'Now, tidy these avay. Now, please!' She gestures to my grandfather's trousers with a disrespectful wave of her hand.

I decide to correct her. To let her know exactly who she's talking to.

'You mean take them off, not tidy them away,' I say smilingly. For I am a young writer, Janet. A writer and a man; a man who has travelled; a lover and a fraud. And if I could I would show you my heart, but it's lost, Janet, lost to one of your cruel kind, Janet. But I will get even, of that much I can assure you!

She questions me with her stupid eyes and I despise her for

her ignorance. For this sad room that she inhabits and the cheapness of her vile, red sling-back shoes. I've no time for such dumbness.

'Oh, forget it!' I say dully and examine my nails.

She turns away confused.

'I get drink for myself!' She curses me in German, turns and walks out.

My heart fills with pride at the superiority of my race. That I should be born English and that I was born a man. Because that's what life is for, isn't it, Janet? To dream and pretend. For me to be your King and for you to be my Queen? Then I kick myself because I should have realised, I should have cottoned on . . . to be polite and not feared, to buy her stinking gut-rot and make-believe. And I call myself a dog and a cad and for not knowing the decency of buying a sweet girl a glass of tipple, even if not a single penny in my pocket is mine.

The door bangs closed behind her and I stand and balk at my idiocy. 'So, you're in a whorehouse now are you, you half-wit? Just like all the greats. A young writer in search of the truth!'

I place my white hands to my pallid brow and stare into the cold mirror. My hair is all wrong, sticking out in mad tufts from under my stupid sailor's hat.

Not very picturesque, a room like this. Narrow, purpose-built. A lonely chair and a dusty sideboard with its broken vase and a yellow plastic rose. A fuck-dungeon.

I don't use the ashtray. Instead I show my contempt and stub out my cigarette on the floor. I sit down gingerly on the edge of the plastic sheet and kick the dog-end under the bed. I step out of my bellbottoms and pull off my jersey.

I check my change and toy with my coins. 'She's been gone at least three minutes now, you oaf! More like four!' I look to the sad plastic rose and count up to five in my head. I tell myself that I have to count to one hundred and fifty out loud before she will return.

I stand up and pace the room. I count in different directions

. . . where are you, my sweet Janet? I tell myself that she's taken my money and run, that I am a stupid fool. 'She's walked out on you because you are a child. You are rude and you are a thug. Listen to me, you scoundrel. Listen to me, I know that you've had sex with a dog!'

I flinch at my harsh words and cower under the stinging accusation, but have to nod in meek agreement that this is indeed the undeniable truth. I harangue myself and call myself all manner of vile names – in short, I goad myself mercilessly.

'Your little Janet's done a runner! You'll get a disease, my friend, a terrible and shameful disease. And all will see the marks emblazoned upon your flesh and know that you had to pay to have a woman, that you are too ugly and unlovable to ever win a real woman's heart!'

I call myself all sorts of outrageous names and taunt myself horribly. One thing's for sure, there's been a big mistake, I've got to leave . . .

I snatch up my combinations and pull them on so quick that I rip off several of the buttons. They *ping!* off and scatter themselves under the dusty bed. I have to find them all, to follow them into the corners, amongst the fluff and grime.

I climb in and out of my bellbottoms several times, sitting on the edge of the plastic sheet, sucking on my cigarette like a lollipop. I stand and walk around the room tormenting myself with glee. I find one fly button right up the back, amongst some used Durex. Actually, I'm on my knees when she walks in and I bang my head. I have to pretend to be examining the rug.

She stands there with her arms folded and her triple gin. I never expected to see her again, but I don't let her know it. My heart overflows with love. For a moment I thought that I'd lost her, that she'd done a runner with my fifty. But she hasn't. Here she is. I stand to kiss her but she just shrugs me off.

'You tidy dis avay! Now! Ten minuten is finished already!' She pulls at my belt.

'Lie downs now please, on zee bed!' She swigs at her gin like a sailor, knocking it back in thirst draughts.

'Please lie downs. I must get dis high!' She wipes her mouth on the back of her hand, turns her back on me, undoes her shorts and steps out of them. She undulates her arse, it springs back, it wobbles then flexes again. I use my eyes like a torch, I reach out, I touch.

'No! You must lies down! Please! I ave to gets dis high!'

She nods grimly towards my centre.

'Please, lies down now, your time is already finished!'

'But we've got half an hour,' I remind her. I trail off, I wanted to get friendly, but apparently it's too late for that now.

'Please! On zee bed, I must get dis high!'

I do as I'm told. I resign myself to suffering. Any minute now and she's gonna throw a wobbler and maybe I won't even be able to lay my sad, hungry, vile eyes upon her beautiful body.

I comply like a puppy dog and lie back on that cold, hateful sheet. Janet opens her purse and rakes through the rubbish for a rubber. I reach out one last time to touch her beautiful arse but she pulls away.

'Lie down! I must get dis fing high!'

She extracts one ... silver foil ... puts her hand to my chest, pushes me down onto the bed, pulls the rubber over my poor little dick. I try to sit up, to reach round for her softness, but she hates me.

'Please! I must get dis high!'

I see no point in arguing and surrender to her aggression.

Ah, Janet, I came here to empty my sorrow, my stinking soul. To search for love in this fragile unknown land. And so I reach out for your softness. Don't bark at me like an angry dog and make me have to lie back on this cold sheet like all the others.

By Jesus Christ, I force myself. I screw up my eyes like tiny fists and hold my breath, to conjure up her existence once more. My lost one, my dear one, my Kursty. And her memory comes running back to me and leaps at my throat with the cold paws of a cat.

Ah, Janet, I need you to hold me, to be her ... to rub out this sadness in my hollow heart.

I reach out and plead, pulling at her hips, to sit her arse on my tongue.

'Stop! I must get zis high! Please ve only have five minutes left!'

I fall back, my hands to my face, my legs twisted in agony. And I laugh at myself out of spite, ridiculing my pain ... teaching myself a lesson. 'My word, you come cheap! To even dare to utter the name of your loved one in this evil place! ... how low can you crawl? No lower, upon my word, you slug! You worm! You treacherous woodlouse!'

I rip into myself with a vengeance and call myself a whore-lover and a dog-fucker with a limp dick! I torture myself mercilessly, until I'm sure that I'm squirming with utter contempt and hating myself with total abandon, with absolute assuredness.

In fact, I don't quit finding fault with myself until I'm in the full knowledge that I am the most wretched and deceitful pervert that ever crawled on the face of this earth; that ever drew breath, even. To be in absolutely no doubts!

'Ah, Janet, with your sad mask painted on, your crayon red lips and thumb print eyes ... I too am wearing a mask, Janet. I too have robbed my soul and thrown the pennies to the street. So, come be with me and we can hunt love together my sad one, because I have lost my love, Janet, and maybe you could be her, or at least pretend to be her, if I bought you ... I am a good man, Janet; you don't know me, but it's true. I shouldn't be here in this worthless place. I should be in a palace emblazoned with jewels and untold riches, and you should be by my side, Janet ... there are girls who could love me and would give themselves to me gratefully if only I would give them the chance ... so let me talk to you, my sweet Janet. Let us leave this sorry room and I will rescue you from this vile night.'

She reaches for my nakedness.

'How much marks you ave?'

I count in my poor troubled head. Of course I have the whole orchestra's bankroll.

'None,' I say.

Her tits sway.

'But I've got my granddad's medals.'

'Vot?'

I lean over and lift my jersey from the floor. Janet turns and looks over her shoulder.

'Is it golds?'

'Silver,' I say. 'Solid silver ... it's his Long Service and Good Conduct Medal.

'I must get dis high first!'

'It's high enough already.'

'Really? Is up enough?'

She turns and looks at me questioningly and I nod in my feeble embarrassment. Janet shakes her head in disbelief then clambers round on the small bed, knocking the sideboard with

her knee. She cocks her leg over my shoulder and lowers her beautiful arse over my face. The little naked light bulb disappears from view.

I see her tits from between her legs as she takes the tip of me into her cold mouth and I stick out my tongue. Her arse twitches, the muscles clench and relax . . . I lie back and stare into her cunt . . . young, denuded, delicate, paid for . . . and it hurts me, and I think of scum, white scum . . . and then I let go, filling the little rubber teat of the Durex. She turns to me, sweeping her hair from her face.

'Over so quick?'

She charms me with her delicate nature, climbs off and skips to the bathroom clasping her little package. I listen for her taking a piss.

I sit up and hold my poor head, then quickly jump to my feet. I drag on my kecks, tuck my little wet pecker away and run. I head off up the corridor, buckling my belt . . . past all the numbers, still pulling my busted shoe on.

'Ay!'

It's my little floozy . . . I don't turn . . . I keep my head down . . . I trip . . . I pull at my laces . . . I hop on one foot, at full gallop.

'Ay!'

She's on my tail, running naked up the corridor . . . her tits bounce . . . I slam into the front door . . . I push and pull on it . . . I kick the handle but it still doesn't budge . . . I whimper to myself, tugging and cursing . . . I feel the dark presence of malevolent forces . . . I grow desperate, clawing at the panelling, my white fingers, the nails chipped . . . Janet shouting her gob off, and I imagine myself a small mouse . . .

'Ay! Du! Halt!'

I can't get it open . . . I turn and grin, my face grown pale. Then the little side door bursts open and the small, mean little pimp shows his scarlet face. Two other fellows peep over his padded shoulders. Dark, square-set, toying with their flick-knives. I have the terrible sensation that I have just jammed a sharp pointed stick into a nest of particularly poisonous and vindictive red ants. They sniff the air with their tiny feelers and flex their poisonous abdomens at me. I let go of the handle and smile. I show them my empty palms.

'A small misunderstanding, gentlemen. Just a little jest, that's all . . . a harmless prank . . . no hard feelings.'

I unpin my grandfather's medal and, pinching a smile at them, walk back down the numbers to my sweet Janet . . . stood there, beautifully naked, her hands on her powerful hips, holding me with her cold eyes. And I want to go down on my knees and thank her for her kindness and for her to punish me for my wickedness. And as I stand recklessly before her she actually looks into my eyes and I pretend that in that split second she realises that she loves me, that she really does care for me.

'You're a liddle bit crazy, no?' She taps the side of her head with her fingers and I nod . . . grinning, yes, always grinning. My colour rising I unpin the medal and hand it to her, tears springing to my eyes . . .

Of course I'm crazy. I'm a young writer. A lover of whores and thieves and good red herring! A man who didn't hide but went out to see the world.

You see, I didn't mean to rob you, Janet. I just wanted for you to hold me and love me. To talk to me and be my friend, even if I do have to pay for it. And somehow, even if deep down inside I do want to break you and have you worship me, it's only because I too am broken, Janet, and cannot love myself.

But I really did want to love you, Janet . . . and to save you . . . and be your friend . . . to give you money . . . to give you everything you ever wished for, Janet. To protect you and promise never to ever let another man lay his filthy stinking rotten hands on your beautiful body ever again!

She glares at me, hot arrows . . . and I look down, shamed by my maleness, by my filthy desires. By my lack of humanity.

And slowly I turn and walk back up past the numbers, waiting to hear her call after me, to hear her bare feet running on the cold linoleum and for me to turn and take her beautiful naked body into my aching arms.

I give those pimps a half smirk . . . I walk on and force myself not to look back, just to show them that I know what I'm about – that I've seen and done this sort of thing a thousand nights before.

I try to put a swing into my broken step, my broken sole flapping . . . the tape useless . . . I hold their gaze, then look away . . . and they dare to laugh at me, those scum!

The little fellow hits the button, smacks his forehead at me and brushes me aside with a gesture of his hands . . . the latch buzzes open and I push the door and step back out into the Hamburg night . . . and I love that chill air with all my heart . . . to be lost in that night . . .

the first one in the boat
kissed the nanny goat
he stroked the nanny
the last one in the boat
had an overcoat of stoat
the nanny kissed his throat
and
all three sang
that'll be that
that'll be that
and all three sang
that'll be that
that'll be that